Teachers Who Thrive

Teachers Who Thrive

Navigating the Self-Efficacy Career Journey

David Grambow

ROWMAN & LITTLEFIELD
Lanham • Boulder • New York • London

Published by Rowman & Littlefield
An imprint of The Rowman & Littlefield Publishing Group, Inc.
4501 Forbes Boulevard, Suite 200, Lanham, Maryland 20706
www.rowman.com

86-90 Paul Street, London EC2A 4NE, United Kingdom

Copyright © 2022 by David Grambow

All rights reserved. No part of this book may be reproduced in any form or by any electronic or mechanical means, including information storage and retrieval systems, without written permission from the publisher, except by a reviewer who may quote passages in a review.

British Library Cataloguing in Publication Information Available

Library of Congress Cataloging-in-Publication Data

Names: Grambow, David, 1971– author.
Title: Teachers who thrive : navigating the self-efficacy career journey / David Grambow.
Description: Lanham, Maryland : Rowman & Littlefield, 2022. | Includes bibliographical references. | Summary: "David Grambow has served as a classroom teacher, technology coach, special educator, principal, and director of instruction. He and his wife have three wonderful children, a backyard full of grandchildren, and a faithful dog, Moose" —Provided by publisher.
Identifiers: LCCN 2022011981 (print) | LCCN 2022011982 (ebook) | ISBN 9781475860801 (cloth) | ISBN 9781475860818 (paperback) | ISBN 9781475860825 (epub)
Subjects: LCSH: Teaching—Vocational guidance—United States. | Teachers—In-service training—United States. | Teachers—Job satisfaction—United States. | Career development—United States.
Classification: LCC LB1775.2 .G727 2022 (print) | LCC LB1775.2 (ebook) | DDC 370.71/1—dc23/eng/20220427
LC record available at https://lccn.loc.gov/2022011981
LC ebook record available at https://lccn.loc.gov/2022011982

DEDICATION

I would like to dedicate this book to all teachers who had their self-efficacy mightily tested by teaching through the COVID-19 pandemic. Your grit and perseverance has inspired me and countless others as you tirelessly faced and conquered the challenges that we could never have predicted. You have reminded the nation of the vital importance of well-supported and efficacious teachers.

Contents

Acknowledgments		ix
Chapter 1	The Transformative Power of Teacher Self-Efficacy	1
Chapter 2	The Five Thrive Factors	9
Chapter 3	The Habits of Thriving Teachers	13
Chapter 4	Focus of Thriving Teachers	33
Chapter 5	The Self-Care Paradox	55
Chapter 6	The Career Stages of a Thriving Teacher	61
Chapter 7	Self-Reflection Career Stages	75
Chapter 8	Feedback Career Stages	97
Chapter 9	Collaboration Career Stages	119
Chapter 10	Student Relationship Career Stages	137
Chapter 11	Inclusive Practice Career Stages	155
Appendix: Thrive Tools		167
Notes		183
About the Author		187

Acknowledgments

This book would not have been possible without the support and inspiration of many very important people in my life. First and foremost, to my wonderful wife, Lori, who persevered through my extended absences as I holed myself up in the basement writing or playing guitar when the words were not flowing. You not only kept me organized and on track in life but you also did the same as I wrote this book. I love you very much.

To Dr. Sarah Noonan, who convinced me I had something worth sharing. Your sage guidance has been a blessing for which I will forever be grateful.

To Andrea Voelker and Erin Schiltgen. Through our collaborative partnership, you both have helped me refine my thinking and operationalize many of the ideas in this book. You also helped me get back on track when my actions were not aligned with the principles contained in these pages. I am grateful for your courageous leadership and advocacy for the profession.

1
The Transformative Power of Teacher Self-Efficacy

If you are reading this book, thank you for what you do every day. You are either a teacher or someone who supports teachers. Great teachers thrive on opening the doors to a limitless future for all their students. These teachers have an unwavering belief in their students' capacity for success. These same teachers must believe in themselves and the skills they need to face the onslaught of challenges aimed in their direction.

Why does teaching feel more challenging to veteran teachers than it did at the beginning of their careers? Why is the teaching shortage reaching crisis levels? Why do teachers begin to experience the ill effects of burnout in as little as five years on the job? The answer to these questions is complex and cannot be fully explored in any one book. Part of the answer, however, is the systematic erosion of teacher self-efficacy.

Teacher self-efficacy is the critical belief teachers have in their ability to successfully execute the vast array of skills necessary to meet the needs of their students. This is a lofty proposition. Schools are expected to do more and more. At the end of the day, a school is only as effective as the teachers who serve there. These increasing expectations for schools translate to higher expectations for teachers. High expectations are critically important, but they need to be accompanied by high levels of support.

The world we live in is becoming more and more divided. Unfortunately, teachers are often thrust in the middle of their community's divisive debates, not because people do not believe in the importance of their work. Rather, they realize, if we are going to work our way out of this mess we find ourselves in, great teachers are key! The misguided and ill-informed attacks on teachers are nothing new. Still, the current climate of discord and blame makes it more challenging to maintain teacher self-efficacy while dealing with the pundits who believe they have the answer in a silver bullet called "reform."

Teachers have been unwillingly thrust into the center of an ongoing political debate. Public education systems often become the front line for addressing social, economic, or cultural challenges faced by our nation. Perspectives change, the challenges evolve, but the constant is the belief by noneducators that these woes can only be "fixed" in the classroom. This is typically cast as "reform." Politicians on both sides of the aisle have been telling teachers directly or through their legislation that what they are doing is not good enough. The politicians' suggestions for reform are often manifest in the form of unfunded mandates and empty promises.

In 1983, the US federal government published *A Nation at Risk: The Imperative for Educational Reform*.[1] *A Nation at Risk* marked a dramatic shift in the perception of public schools in America. For the first time in history, Americans called into question the global preeminence of our K–12 school system. *A Nation at Risk*, however, called into question the effectiveness of our *educational institution*, not necessarily *teachers*. Nearly thirty years later, a new chapter in politically based education reform has emerged at the state level due to increasingly insidious political polarization.

Research tells us teacher effectiveness is the most critical factor related to student achievement and growth. This critical understanding should empower teachers to embrace their potential transformational impact. Instead, critics have turned the tables and argued that a lack of teacher accountability has chipped away at our global competitive edge. This dynamic has played out in various ways throughout communities and states, often plunging schools and teachers in the middle of political maneuverings that have little to do with student learning.

From the landmark Elementary and Secondary Education Act of 1965 to its reauthorization as No Child Left Behind (2001) and then the Every Student Succeeds Act (2015), school reform efforts have been established with the best of intentions. States have taken up the mantle of school reform as well. For example, on March 11, 2011, Wisconsin Governor Scott Walker signed Act 10, otherwise known as the Budget Repair Bill.[2]

Act 10 engendered significant controversy and became a lightning rod for vitriol and division. Supporters of Act 10 asserted that the bill effectively addressed a considerable budget deficit. Critics of the law claimed Governor Walker was attempting to balance the budget at the expense of public school teachers. I personally saw both benefits and risks associated with this bill. Many teachers felt a loss of support when reform efforts were aimed at teacher effectiveness.

Supporters of the legislation viewed it as a commonsense reform measure to control school spending and provide districts the flexibility to address their financial needs and balance their budgets. Act 10 limited union rights for collective bargaining and shifted commitments to pensions and insurance from the state to the district and to teachers. Many teachers interpreted the debates and community-wide arguments regarding the merits of Act 10 as a direct questioning of the value of public education and public school teachers. Wisconsin teachers found themselves in a political maelstrom.

As an elementary principal at the time, I understood the benefits and challenges of Act 10, but my understanding had no tangible impact on my next steps. I had a responsibility to find a way to empower teachers to rebound and embrace their power to meet the needs of all our students. Unfortunately, some teachers felt so discouraged that their passion for teaching eroded. Although disappointed in the political landscape, some teachers remained focused on their students and ignored disparaging comments about the value of public education, which cast doubt on their effectiveness.

Teacher self-efficacy is a critical and often overlooked aspect of overall teacher effectiveness. Teacher effectiveness studies document the vital role teachers play in student success. Additionally, research has demonstrated a strong correlation between teacher self-efficacy and teacher effectiveness. Essentially, a teacher cannot maximize their impact on students if they do not believe in their own talents and skills. Teachers' beliefs in their abilities are always critical, but the importance is underscored amid crisis. There are abundant forces at work relentlessly sending us messages implying we are not doing enough. Self-efficacy helps teachers stave off the pervasive harmful influence of these negative messages.

Teachers who thrive are undoubtedly efficacious. They thrive in large part because they believe in their abilities and refuse to relinquish their agency. Teachers who thrive, however, also must find balance in their lives. High levels of self-efficacy can be a burden if they are not tempered by a balanced perspective recognizing the need for self-care.

This book is designed as a travel guide through your professional journey toward sustainable and vibrant self-efficacy. In the following pages, you will read the stories of a diverse group of teachers. Some of these teachers started their careers with abundant self-efficacy. Others learned how to develop their self-efficacy later in their careers. Some found ways to balance their drive to reach all students with an equal measure of care for their families and themselves. Sadly, you will read about a few teachers who could not find that balance and ultimately succumbed to the all-too-common affliction of teacher burnout. Additionally, you will have the opportunity to reflect on your self-efficacy and learn strategies to grow throughout your career continually.

Now, more than ever, we need highly efficacious teachers at all career stages. This book is designed as a tool for improvement with a built-in study guide. As you read the book, you will be presented with stories, reflective questions, and challenges to engage you in the content. Whether you are a teacher interested in increasing your self-efficacy, a leader who wants to leverage the transformative power of teacher self-efficacy, or a group focused on harnessing collective efficacy, the stories you read will form the basis for your exploration of discovery and improvement. I invite you to turn the next page in this book as you turn the next page in your journey toward a thriving career.

THE ROOTS OF TEACHER SELF-EFFICACY

To thrive is to continually grow and flourish. So why do some teachers thrive throughout their teaching careers while others succumb to the pressures of the job? Why do some teachers positively address challenges in their schools while others find it impossible to ride the wave of continual change? The answer, in large part, is teacher self-efficacy.

This book is based on a simple premise. Teacher self-efficacy changes children's lives. Teachers with the belief in their abilities to harness the transformative power of excellent instruction can permanently alter the trajectory for their career and, subsequently, their students' lives. It is imperative that we do everything we can to support an essential resource we have to transform our schools: teachers who thrive. Teachers who thrive are more impactful than any new curricular resource, political initiative, or shiny new technology-based innovation.

This book offers a roadmap for teachers on the self-efficacy journey at any stage in their career. To create this roadmap, we must first begin with a fundamental understanding of self-efficacy and, more specifically, teacher self-efficacy. Albert Bandura is the uncontested forefather of self-efficacy theory. Bandura initially described the concept of self-efficacy as part of his Social Cognitive Theory.[3] Bandura defined self-efficacy as "People's judgments of their capabilities to organize and execute courses of action required to attain designated types of performances."[4] Other scholars later advanced this knowledge by conducting empirical studies focusing on specific aspects of self-efficacy.

Bandura theorized that human learning occurs through complex reciprocal interactions among the person, the environment, and behavior. His theory stood in stark contrast to a strict behavioral model which held that learning occurs only due to external stimuli without accounting for the social aspects of learning nor the person's past learning experiences. Self-efficacy is an important construct within Social Cognitive Theory or SCT. It speaks specifically to an individual's belief in their abilities and their influence on learning and performance.

BANDURA'S FOUR SOURCES OF SELF-EFFICACY

Bandura identified four sources of self-efficacy. These include: mastery experiences, vicarious experiences, social persuasion, and physiological or emotional states. These four sources form the cornerstone of the practical pursuit of self-efficacy. The sources are context-specific, meaning how teachers access these sources and develop self-efficacy is different from any other profession. Bandura continued to study self-efficacy in specific contexts and synthesized the work of other scholars in later editions of his books and articles. His work laid the foundation for future scholars to explore the ways in which self-efficacy impacts teachers' effectiveness and job satisfaction.

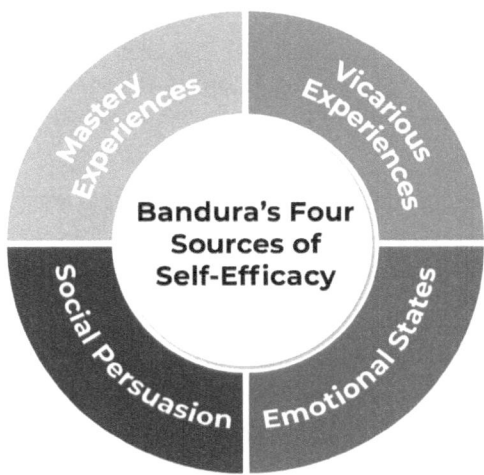

Bandura's Four Sources of Self-Efficacy.[5]

When individuals consistently perform a task well, they may increase self-efficacy because of the results of a "mastery experience." Mastery experiences are the most direct and impactful source of self-efficacy. For teachers, mastery experiences could include successfully implementing a new instructional strategy or facilitating a breakthrough with a student.

Vicarious experiences are those in which the participant witnesses the process and change in others who have developed a sense of mastery. Gaining self-efficacy through vicarious experiences underscores the importance of collaboration in the development of self-efficacy. Teachers are not alone in their quest to develop self-efficacy. Strong professional learning communities serve as superb avenues for teachers to gain self-efficacy through vicarious experiences.

The third source, social persuasion, describes the way positive reinforcement from others can build self-efficacy. Social persuasion is a critical source for teachers as teachers naturally want to support one another. Social persuasion is another source predicated on collaboration. Mentoring and instructional coaching are wonderful opportunities to maximize social persuasion in efforts to develop self-efficacy.

Emotional or physiological states describe internal experiences that create feelings that encourage participants to believe in themselves and their abilities. This source is often overlooked. Teachers primarily pursue their career choices based on their passion. Teachers overwhelmingly describe "lightbulb" moments when they facilitate a breakthrough for a student as the highlights of their day. This emotional feeling teachers experience during lightbulb moments can fuel their self-efficacy.

These sources are interconnected as they often work in conjunction with one another. For example, a teacher may successfully implement a new math intervention, generating a mastery experience that elicits an emotional response. Both the mastery experience and the emotional response fuel the teacher's self-efficacy. Teacher self-efficacy is complex and multifaceted. Accordingly, the four sources impact self-efficacy by bolstering any of the three components of teacher self-efficacy.

COMPONENTS OF TEACHER SELF-EFFICACY

To further define self-efficacy in educational settings, Tschannen-Moran and Woolfolk Hoy developed a widely accepted definition of teacher self-efficacy: "A teacher's judgment of his or her ability to positively impact engagement and learning for all students regardless of the challenges they may present."[6] They found teachers can demonstrate their self-efficacy through three specific domains, including instruction, student engagement, and classroom management.

As described previously, self-efficacy is context- and skill-specific: teachers may not be equally efficacious in two different settings with two different tasks. Teacher self-efficacy comprises teachers' self-efficacy and their knowledge and skills associated with effective teaching. Scholars and practitioners have since expanded our understanding and application of teacher self-efficacy in countless ways.

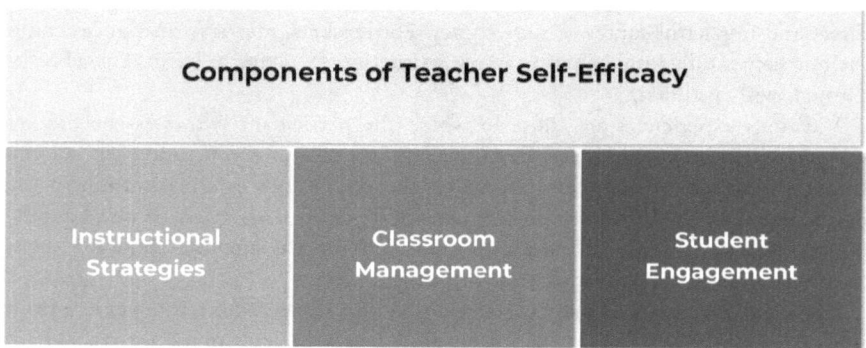

Three Components of Teacher Self-Efficacy. Megan Tschannen-Moran and Anita Woolfolk-Hoy. "Three Components of Teacher Self-Efficacy." Adapted from "Teacher Efficacy: Capturing an Elusive Construct." *Teaching and Teacher Education* 17(7): 783–805. (2001). doi:https://doi.org/10.1016/s0742-051x(01)00036-1.[7]

Teachers who thrive not only have high levels of self-efficacy related to instruction, classroom management, and engagement—they also feel efficacious in their ability to practice self-care strategies. Without this fourth critical element, we run the risk of holding ourselves to a mythical superhero level of teaching that is not sustainable nor healthy. In order to take the best care of our students, we must be able to take care of ourselves.

This book is designed to operate as a self-guided study in the development of self-efficacy throughout a career. It is filled with opportunities to reflect on the concepts contained in the following pages, not simply read about them. Whether you are a teacher interested in applying these concepts by yourself or you work as someone who supports teachers and their professional development, you will be presented opportunities to dig in!

Each section will begin with a short vignette about a teacher who exemplifies certain aspects of the thrive framework. The vignette will be preceded by "Activators," which are designed to activate your schema and prepare you to key in on the critical aspects of the story. The vignette will be followed by reflective questions and a thrive challenge designed to get you out of your comfort zone and into the learning zone. We use theories and models to explain and understand complex ideas and phenomena. For each of the "Five Thrive Factors," we will use a theory or two to more thoroughly understand the factor. Sometimes people view theories as pedantic academia lacking opportunity for practical application. On the contrary, theory, when used appropriately, allows us to analyze our practices and professional circumstances more thoroughly.

THE JOURNEY TO A THRIVING CAREER

As you prepare to explore this book, let's take a moment to set the stage. The title of this book, *Teachers Who Thrive: Navigating the Self-Efficacy Career Journey*, intentionally invokes images of travel. Building a thriving teaching career holds many parallels to travel. Just like travel, we must forge our path when developing a thriving career.

As you will see in the upcoming pages, the discussion of Thrive Factors is designed to serve as your travel guide. Just like planning a trip, you are not expected to jump into your journey without knowing where you are heading. Are you looking for fun in the sun or a guided historical tour through Eastern Europe? Are you looking for adventure or renewal? Are you traveling with friends, by yourself, or with your family? It would help if you had opportunities to understand your potential destinations to find a match between your trip and your personal goals. Chapters 1 through 4 will provide you with the background necessary to plan the next phase of your journey.

Once you have an idea of what you hope to accomplish during a trip, it is time to begin planning your journey. Chapters 5 through 11 serve as your itinerary for your trip toward a thriving teaching career. As teachers progress through their careers, they access each of the Five Thrive Factors in different ways. In these chapters, you will learn which phase you currently operate in with regard to each of the Five Thrive Factors. You will also learn how you can advance to the next phase to maximize your self-efficacy. The process of mapping out your self-efficacy journey is very personal. No two teacher journeys are alike. This discussion will allow you to deepen your understanding of your pathway.

Once you have decided on your destination and mapped your journey, it is time to pack your luggage. If you are off to Hawaii, do not forget your sunscreen. If you are heading to Paris, remember your tickets to the Louvre. You will learn how to pack for your journey toward a thriving teaching career. You will find tools you can use individually or collaboratively to develop your self-efficacy continuously. You also will discover protocols for professional learning community dialogue, rubrics for evaluating related practices, and inventories to measure your current levels of teacher self-efficacy. I invite you now to turn the page and take that single step on your journey.

2
The Five Thrive Factors

Think about this section as your personal travel guide you use to plan for a thriving career. When planning a trip, you typically would not fire up Google Maps and begin plotting your adventure. Instead, you likely would want to learn about the destination by exploring points of interest, highlights, and a bit about the history. Once you have immersed yourself in the content of your travel guide, you are ready to break out the map and chart your journey. Early chapters will provide you with the highlights and points of interest about each Thrive Factor through the vignettes, a brief theory overview, and reflection opportunities. In subsequent chapters, you will begin to chart your efficacious career journey.

As you will learn in the subsequent pages, self-reflection critically supports the development of teacher self-efficacy. To that end, the structure of this chapter allows you to reflect as you read. Each segment dedicated to one of the Five Thrive Factors will include five sections, including stories, reflection questions, and opportunities to connect the learning to your practice.

Activators set the stage by allowing you to engage your background knowledge by responding to open-ended questions and exploring your understanding of the topic at hand. *Vignettes* are short stories designed to place the Thrive Factor in a real-life context. *Thrive Theories* present a brief exploration of a pertinent theory that helps us understand the Thrive Factor more thoroughly. The *Application to Practice* section provides an opportunity to connect the lessons of the vignette and the theory to your practice. Interspersed, you will find a variety of reflection questions. At the end of each section, you will be allowed to step outside of your comfort zone and consider a *Thrive Challenge*, which is designed to encourage you to operationalize the learning. If you choose to conduct a book study with *Teachers Who Thrive*, all you need to do is assign the sections and begin reading. Enjoy your journey toward a thriving and rewarding career!

The Five Thrive Factors

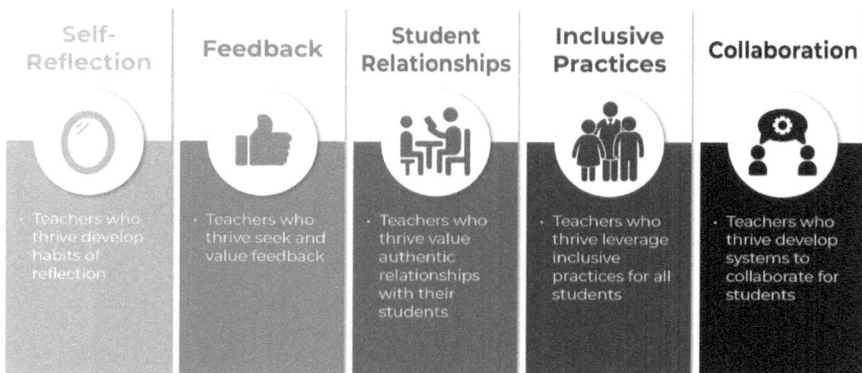

The Five Thrive Factors. David Grambow. *The Five Thrive Factors*. 2021.

The Five Thrive Factors serve as the vehicles you will use to traverse your course toward a rewarding career where you continually grow as you refine your ability to reach all of your students. Teachers engage these factors in a variety of ways. The manner in which teachers engage in these factors is as diverse as the teachers themselves. Every teacher will naturally gravitate to one or more of these factors. Other factors may manifest as limiting factors for specific teachers. Teachers who thrive find ways to leverage their natural strengths and deliberately address their relative weaknesses. But, as we will learn, teachers who thrive also temper their enthusiasm for constant professional growth by recognizing the need to take care of themselves, their families, and their friends.

These five factors work interdependently. For instance, feedback can inspire self-reflection and engaging in inclusive practices such as co-teaching requires meaningful collaboration. Again, every teacher's journey toward a thriving career may be unique, but the five factors we will explore in this chapter will undoubtedly be a part of the journey.

The first three factors are the habits of thriving teachers. They include self-reflection, feedback, and collaboration. These habits represent the cognitive predispositions that fuel self-efficacy. These habits exist to various degrees in all teachers but, more importantly, can be learned, developed, honed, and mastered. If you can internalize these three habits, you will be well on your way to a rewarding and thriving career.

The second two factors represent the focus of thriving teachers. They include a focus on student relationships and a focus on inclusive practices. Teachers who remain committed to continuous development in these two focus areas bolster their teacher self-efficacy, allowing them to thrive. By applying the habits of thriving teachers to these focus areas, teachers are in the driver's seat of their careers.

Through the course of your exploration of this section, you will understand how the Five Thrive Factors support all teachers. You will have opportunities to reflect on your relationship with these five factors. Additionally, you will learn some quick strategies to strengthen your teacher self-efficacy irrespective of your years of experience.

Each of the Five Thrive Factors contains subcategories that will assist you in understanding how you can access the factors. These subcategories are consistently available to teachers regardless of their years of experience. The next chapter explicitly addresses the power of self-reflection in building self-efficacy. You will explore the differences between formal reflective practices and reflection-in-action. Like travel, planning for a great experience is critical and can be almost as rewarding as the journey itself. Bon Voyage!

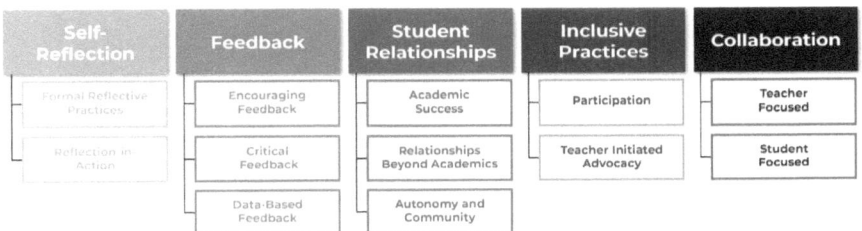

Thrive Factors and Subcategories. David Grambow. *Five Thrive Factors and Subcategories*. 2021.

3

The Habits of Thriving Teachers

Some people love to travel. They live to travel! These folks usually share some habits in common with one another that allow them to enjoy their travel while minimizing the associated stressors. They tend to plan, practice adaptability, and communicate openly. These habits pave the way for successful travel. When you embark on your thriving teacher journey, a few habits will help you along the way. These habits are the first three Thrive Factors. They include self-reflection, seeking and valuing feedback, and collaboration.

SELF-REFLECTION ACTIVATORS

The vignette you will read shortly explores the power of intentional reflection. It examines the reflective habits of Caroline, an elementary teacher who is thoroughly dedicated to her students. She, like Professor Dumbledore, employs metacognition or thinking about her own thinking to improve her practice.

- How would you describe your reflective habits?
- Do you reflect on your professional and personal life? If so, which do you do more? Why?
- Are you aware you are reflecting when you reflect?
- What conditions make it easier for you to engage in meaningful reflection?

SELF-REFLECTION VIGNETTE: CAROLINE AND THE PENSIEVE

Professor Dumbledore, Harry Potter's headmaster at Hogwarts and renowned teacher in the wizarding world created by J. K. Rowling, understood the value of reflection to his self-efficacy. Dumbledore used his Pensieve, a magical vessel used to store and revisit memories, to aid in his reflection. Dumbledore explained, "I use the Pensieve. One simply siphons the excess thoughts from one's mind . . . and examines them at one's leisure. It becomes easier to spot patterns and links."[1] The Pensieve is an example of Rowling's genius play on words—in this case, three words.

The first word Rowling incorporated into her wizardly wordplay was "pensive," which means to engage in meaningful reflection. The second word she included was "sieve," meaning, quite simply, a strainer. Finally, there is the word itself spelled slightly differently, "pensieve," meaning engaged in deep thought. Rowling used this whimsical metaphor to describe Dumbledore's recognition of the importance of sifting, categorizing, and analyzing past events to develop new and impactful understandings. Teachers in the Muggle world engage in this same sort of reflective practice every day. The following vignette tells the story of a teacher and instructional coach who relies on self-reflection as an evolving art bolstering her self-efficacy at every turn.

Caroline worked as an instructional coach in an elementary school. She spent the first sixteen years of her career as a classroom teacher. Caroline's colleagues and principal consider her a highly efficacious teacher. In an interview, she shared a detailed and vivid account of her reflective practices, the factor she felt most directly impacted her self-efficacy development.

Caroline was always reflective. As a child, she fastidiously maintained a diary where she would reflect on the day's happenings. She described this diary as filled with "99% pure monotony." However, the one percent protected her innermost secrets and insights into events and milestones that turned out to be significant to creating the amazing teacher she had become.

As a teacher, Caroline made it a point to journal about her practice frequently. Thoughts about professional development, ideas for upcoming lessons, and quips about kids who lightened her spirit all filled the pages of her journal. "My journal has been important to me, but honestly, I rarely go back and read what I wrote. It is the thinking by writing that is important to me," Caroline shared.

As Caroline's responsibilities at home and work mounted, the habit of reflecting through journaling suffered. So did her self-efficacy. She found herself thrown off her game by relatively insignificant bumps along her teaching journey. She lost her Pensieve. She no longer capitalized on the process of sifting through her thoughts and making sense of her busy day. Caroline began considering leaving the profession.

On a whim, Caroline and her husband spent a weekend at a spa as a way to reconnect with one another and carve out some time to rejuvenate. So she signed up for a class on mantra meditation. Mantra meditation involves focusing on a word or short phrase to transcend conscious thought and open your mind. Caroline thoroughly enjoyed the meditation experience, but she had not yet realized the full benefit of meditation.

Later that evening, while getting ready for dinner, Caroline found herself in a place she had not been in a long time. She was actively reflective and able to clearly de-scramble the swirling thoughts that never quite came to the surface. She found her Pensieve once again. Caroline committed herself to meditate, thus changing her personal and professional trajectory.

Meditation allowed Caroline to reconnect with the power of intentional self-reflection. As a result, she incorporated meditation into her daily routine. Shortly after her meditation revelation, Caroline resumed her journaling routine. Journaling coupled with meditation boosted Caroline's self-efficacy significantly. As a result, she pursued and accepted a position as an instructional coach where she had the opportunity to work with other teachers to increase their reflective capacity. Much like Dumbledore, Caroline is now committed to unleashing the capacity of teachers and students to whom she so selflessly dedicates herself.

SELF-REFLECTION THEORY: HALL AND SIMERAL'S CONTINUUM OF SELF-REFLECTION

As we begin exploring this first theory, let us take a moment to reflect on the rationale for including theories as part of our exploration. Esteemed social psychologist Kurt Lewin once aptly and famously said, "There's nothing so practical as a good theory."[2] Theory allows us to be creative by applying a system of ideas to whatever context we are considering. If this book were filled with nothing more than concrete examples, a reader could certainly replicate each example.

Theories, however, allow us to create our research-grounded practices and programs by extrapolating the lessons we learn from examples. We will use concrete examples to deepen our understanding in this book, but the marriage of theory and practice provides much more fertile cognitive soil for cultivating. Pete Hall and Alisa A. Simeral developed an amazingly effective theoretical model that certainly advances our understanding of reflection.

Hall and Simeral's Continuum of Self-Reflection serves as a framework to enhance our understanding of levels of teacher self-reflection.[3] The Continuum of Self-Reflection categorizes the level of a teacher's reflective capacity in one of four stages: unaware, conscious, action, and refinement. Hall and Simeral also offer practical strategies for a teacher, coach, or administrator to move toward the next stage. I truly appreciate the optimism Hall and Simeral infused into this model. The fact that they conceptualize stages implies the ability to progress to the next stage as opposed to labels that denote an evaluative finality.

Teachers in the *Unaware Stage* may not be cognizant of the needs of their students. They tend to focus on the routine of teaching, not the outcomes for students. Additionally, "unaware" teachers often limit their collaboration to superficial and low-impact interactions. To move to the next level on the self-reflection continuum, teachers at the unaware stage must individually or collaboratively increase their understanding of the need for change on behalf of their students.

Teachers in the *Conscious Stage* recognize a need but lack the self-efficacy to believe they have the ability to address the concern. Teachers in this stage demonstrate a disconnect between what they know and what they do. They understand best-practice strategies but do not consistently embed them into their practice. For teachers in the conscious stage, consistency is the name of the game. To move to the next level, they must more deliberately and consistently apply their knowledge of best practice.

Teachers in the *Action Stage* can reflect on their teaching strategies and plan to improve student outcomes. Teachers at this stage embrace the power of self-efficacy. They accept their responsibility for the learning of their students. These teachers move to the next stage by leveraging their experiences and expertise to add to their toolbox of strategies.

Teachers at the *Refinement Stage* personalize their efforts and create specific plans for all students based on individual needs. Once teachers reach this stage, they have become perpetual motion machines of reflective power. As a result, they are often highly efficacious and continually reflect on their actions that contribute to student learning. This reflection leads to an even more refined strategic focus on their students.[4]

As you read briefly about Hall and Simeral's model, how did it align with what you know about reflection?

Hall & Simeral's Continuum of Self-Reflection

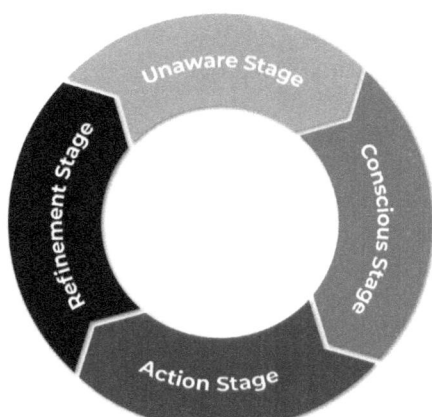

Hall and Simeral's Continuum of Self-Reflection. Peter Hall and Alison Simeral. Building Teachers' Capacity for Success a Collaborative Approach for Coaches and School Leaders (Alexandria, VA: Association for Supervision and Curriculum Development, 2008), p 31.[5]

SELF-REFLECTION: APPLICATION TO PRACTICE

We have explored the story of Caroline, an expert reflector, and we have learned about Hall and Simeral's framework for teacher reflection. Now it is time to turn our attention inward and plan for your self-efficacy development. We will examine two forms of reflection that you can employ to unleash your self-efficacy. They are formal reflective practice and reflection-in-action.

Formal versus Casual Reflective Practices: Formal reflective practices are those that teachers systematize and make part of their regular planning process. In the previous vignette, Caroline engaged in highly formal reflective practices, including an almost ritualized meditation practice to engage in deep reflection. Formal reflective practices could include a scheduled meeting with a coach, a nightly phone call with a trusted collegial friend, or a daily journaling habit.

On the opposite side of that continuum lies casual reflective practices. At the most extreme, these practices are so casual that the teacher is unaware they are reflecting. These practices often involve quiet thought but no documentation. You may know you are a casual reflector if your best ideas come to you in the shower! There is no value judgment involved here. Very advanced reflective practitioners can either engage in very formal or very casual practice and everything in between.

The reflective practices described thus far all occurred at the end of the day or workweek. In other cases, formal reflection can be a naturally recursive process during the actual teaching experience. For instance, a highly collaborative PLC (professional learning community) team might use their time together to reflect on their results formally. In addition, some teachers find brief reflective conversations during passing time enough to spark creativity and encourage instructional adjustments.

Reflection-in-Action versus Reflection-on-Action: The formal reflective practices we explored all take place after a learning experience. Reflection-in-action, however, takes place during the teaching and learning experience.[6] This sort of reflection requires advanced expertise due to the necessity of quick thinking. If teachers are not extremely familiar with the content and instructional strategies being employed, it could be overwhelming to consider reflection-in-action.

We can conceptualize reflection-in-action as "thinking on our feet" with deliberate and focused intent. For a teacher, this might look like reading the room and realizing an instructional adjustment is necessary. However, it could also look like a teacher "working the room" by circulating and responding immediately to gaps in understanding.

Reflection-on-action is slightly less responsive as it takes place after the action or teaching experience. When reflecting on action, we are asking questions such as, "What would I do differently next time?" or "What can I learn from this experience?" This reflection is just as crucial as reflection-in-action as it opens up opportunities to share these reflective experiences in a collaborative setting. If we are only focused on reflection-in-action, we are solitary reflectors. I strongly recommend seeking opportunities to reflect both in-action and on-action for maximum thrive potential.

Leveraging Reflection: How do we leverage what we know about the power of self-reflection to increase our self-efficacy? The answer to this question is where the rubber hits the road. We will start by revisiting the story of highly reflective Caroline. The reflective habits highlighted in Caroline's vignette from her childhood diary to her meditation practices would be classified as "formal reflection."

Based on the vignette, we can be certain Caroline is at least in the *Action Stage*, if not the *Refinement Stage* of Hall and Simeral's continuum. Caroline demonstrates the telltale mark of a teacher in the *Action Stage*. She uses her reflective revelations to change her practice and improve student learning. However, until we know more about her use of reflection to personalize her instruction for individual students, we will not be able to discern if she is at the *Refinement Stage*.

Now is our opportunity to examine our reflective strengths and habits. The following four questions will help identify at which stage you generally operate as a reflective educator:

1. How regularly do you think about your teaching and adjust your instruction?

Your response to this question will help you determine your general use of intentional reflection, a prerequisite for effective formal reflection or reflection-in-action. If you find you cannot readily identify your reflection frequency, you likely will benefit by increasing your deliberate reflection. Implementing some weekly formal reflective practices could be a great place to start. For example, consider journaling, chatting with trusted colleagues, or dedicating quiet reflection time you could fit into your daily routine.

Operating beyond the conscious stage is not likely if you do not regularly and intentionally reflect on your teaching. By increasing your reflective practices, you will likely be able to affect some mini-breakthroughs through which you can overcome a knowing-doing gap. If you have access to an instructional coach, by all means, utilize their expertise. Most instructional coaches have training and skills in developing reflective habits.

2. Do you have reflection routines that you follow every week, every day, or every class period?

This question is a simple one allowing you to evaluate formal reflective practices and your reflection-in-action. Although formal reflection can be highly effective, reflection-in-action holds the most transformative capacity. With reflection-in-action, you can more easily personalize instruction, and you can certainly operate at the refinement stage in the Continuum of Self-Reflection.

3. When you reflect and adjust your instruction, do you implement the adjustments the next time you teach the lesson, on follow-up lessons, or during the lesson?

This question will help you identify the degree to which you engage in reflection-in-action. It also provides preliminary insight into your level of self-reflection on

Hall and Simeral's continuum. If you come to realize that you deliberately engage in reflection and make adjustments while teaching, you are likely leveraging reflection-in-action. If you are adjusting instruction for follow-up lessons, you are likely at least operating at the action stage on the Continuum of Self-Reflection.

If you find it difficult to answer this question, you may need to consider adopting formal reflection habits. It is not uncommon for teachers to engage in reflective practices without being fully aware. This, of course, is better than not reflecting at all, but it is not ideal. By engaging in some formal reflective practices, you will establish habits that will allow you to understand your reflective tendencies more metacognitively.

4. How ready are you to address issues that you uncover while you reflect?

This question speaks directly to the self-efficacy building capacity of reflection. If the conditions for high-quality reflection are met, you can experience a significant boost to your self-efficacy. We are looking for those moments when you think about student responses to your instruction and the lightbulb bursts to life. Your creativity is sparked, and ideas begin flowing so quickly you scramble for a Post-it note or the back of a receipt to capture your ideas. You cannot wait until you are back with your students and able to try out your new ideas. This empowerment is indicative of well-honed self-reflective practices likely at the refinement stage on the Continuum of Self-Reflection. It is worth noting that this sort of empowering reflection can be formal reflection or reflection-in-action.

As we have learned, self-reflection serves as a significant contributor to teacher self-efficacy. Self-reflection is absolutely foundational as it creates the pathways for you to employ the other factors we will explore in subsequent sections. Remember that you have been trained. You have experienced exceptional professional learning opportunities. You have learned from and with fantastic colleagues. You are the most valuable asset to your school and your students. And finally, you are the most important asset you have on your journey toward a thriving career.

SELF-REFLECTION: REFLECTION QUESTIONS

- Based on what you have learned, how do you describe your current reflective practices?
- How could you enhance your reflective practices?
- Think of instances when your reflection has led to insight that changed your practice. What elements of the reflective practice made it impactful?
- How could you enhance the reflective capacity of a colleague?
- How can you leverage self-reflection to ensure you are maintaining a work-life balance?

SELF-REFLECTION THRIVE CHALLENGE

Maintain a self-reflection journal for two weeks. Each day, write or record for five minutes responding to the following questions:

- What went well today?
- What could have gone better?
- Which student(s) need more of my attention tomorrow?
- What will that attention look like?

Begin each day by briefly reviewing your journal entry. Then, at the end of the two-week period, examine your reflection, looking for themes and potential next steps.

Now that you have a firm understanding of the role of self-reflection in developing your teacher self-efficacy, we will harness those self-reflective skills as we explore the other four contributing factors. Next, we will explore the power of feedback.

FEEDBACK ACTIVATORS

The following vignette highlights the career of famed math teacher Jaime Escalante. If you were exploring a career in education in the 1980s, you probably knew at least a bit about Mr. Escalante. As you read his story, consider the following questions:

- What do you already know about Mr. Escalante?
- How does the desire drive you as a teacher?
- How do you respond emotionally when you read about Mr. Escalante's teaching?
- What sources of feedback does Mr. Escalante receive?

FEEDBACK VIGNETTE: GANAS Y CREENCIA (DESIRE AND BELIEF)

The late 1980s provided a treasure trove of inspirational teacher movies. Hollywood released two blockbusters in back-to-back years. Robin Williams starred in *Dead Poets Society*, released in 1989, and moved many aspiring teachers to believe in the transformational power of strong teacher-student relationships.[7] One year earlier, *Stand and Deliver* introduced the world to Jaime Escalante and the remarkable success of his students.[8] Jaime Escalante approached his craft in an innovative and unorthodox manner that certainly ruffled some establishment feathers. However, Mr. Escalante's story demonstrates the impact feedback can have on teacher self-efficacy.

Escalante embarked on his journey toward national acclaim at Garfield High School in East Los Angeles. However, he was not new to teaching. He taught for several years in his native country, Bolivia, before pursuing his dreams of opportunities in the United States. It was, however, at Garfield where Escalante refined his philosophy. Escalante came to believe that all it took was *ganas*, or desire, for students to succeed in an extremely challenging course such as Advanced Placement (AP) calculus.

Garfield High School did not have a history of strong academic achievement. When Escalante joined the staff, he did not sense that Garfield's culture embraced a belief in the students and their ability to succeed. Garfield's principal, Henry Gradillas, described the school when he joined the staff as an underperforming school plagued with a sense of apathy. Most Garfield students were Latinx kids from middle- to low-income backgrounds. These were kids accustomed to being marginalized and being left alone if they were not causing trouble. Gang violence surrounded and infiltrated the school. Escalante had his work cut out for him.

Escalante assumed an unwavering approach and maintained high expectations for his students. He did not believe in programs for gifted students dependent on entrance tests. He did not believe in programs that limited participation based on previous performance. He believed in ganas. Escalante believed students need to want deeply to succeed. Escalante believed in any student with the desire to work hard. He also believed in himself. He authoritatively believed he could "make" students succeed.[9] This may be a bit direct for some tastes, but he certainly believed in his abilities.

Eventually, the tenacity of Escalante and his students paid off. Escalante's students amassed an impressive track record of success in Advanced Placement Calculus. In 1987, students at Garfield High completed 129 AP Calculus exams with an impressive 66% passing rate with scores of 3 or above. Only three schools in the United States administered more exams, and those three did not face the systemic challenges at Garfield.[10]

It goes without saying that Mr. Escalante and his students thrived. Escalante had a deep belief in his ability to help students of all backgrounds achieve at the highest level. This belief was supported by feedback from several sources. He relied on feedback from administrators, peers, and students.

With all the bravado Escalante portrayed, behind the scenes, he had his doubts. Upon accepting the position at Garfield, he quickly considered asking for his computer technician job back as he doubted his ability to succeed. Henry Gradillas, Escalante's principal, offered the kind of feedback Escalante craved. Gradillas trusted teachers and wanted to remove barriers to innovation. Gradillas offered encouraging feedback in its most simple form. He wanted to know what Escalante planned on accomplishing and let him know to trust his instincts.

Escalante credits much of his success to the support of Gradillas. Gradillas himself said, "Sometimes the best thing an administrator can do is get out of the way . . . of good teachers."[11] Get out of the way he did, along with providing supportive feedback. In a personal conversation with Dr. Gradillas, he spoke of the challenges and pushback he received as he offered feedback that freed up his teachers to pursue excellence when that pursuit was not necessarily aligned to the traditional practices of his district. Not only did his supportive feedback boost Mr. Escalante's self-efficacy, it also supported his self-efficacy as a school administrator.

Escalante relied on an even more impactful source of feedback, his students. In 1982, ETS, the testing company that scores AP exams, accused Garfield High, and by extension, Escalante's students, of cheating. Escalante was incensed. He believed the accusation was racially motivated. He felt the big corporation could not believe a bunch of kids with Latin surnames could achieve at such impressive levels.

ETS offered Escalante's students the opportunity to retake the exam. There were several risks involved in this decision. This case was receiving national attention. If, by chance, the class did not do as well, it could call their progress and accomplishments into question and destroy the collective belief in their ability they had so deservedly amassed. Escalante had already developed a habit of seeking feedback from his students. From his call-and-response chant about ganas, passersby could hear bellowing from his class to engaging in meaningful dialogue about what was working and what was not working for his students; Escalante relied on his students' feedback to fuel his self-efficacy.

Now it was time to turn to student feedback in a different form. He asked each student about their desire to retake the test. Weeks of grueling inquisition ensued that went as far as administering polygraphs to students allowing them to prove they were telling the truth. The students spoke of their belief in themselves that was unequivocally fostered by Escalante's belief in them, and, by extension, his belief in himself. Escalante turned his classroom into a high-efficiency self-efficacy production machine.

This efficacy garnered results. The students decided to retake the test. Based on their needs, Escalated provided targeted instruction. They not only proved the results were valid, but their retakes also outshined their previous results. Escalante and his students were the real deal. This success supported by meaningful feedback most certainly fueled the self-efficacy of Jaime Escalante and his extraordinary students. We can use established theory to make sense of the way feedback contributed to Escalante's feedback. More importantly, we can understand how feedback can impact our self-efficacy or the efficacy of the teachers we support.

FEEDBACK THEORY: EFFECTIVE TEACHER FEEDBACK FRAMEWORK

In late 1964, the Beatles changed the future of rock and roll when John Lennon carelessly leaned his guitar against Paul McCartney's bass amplifier. Paul plucked the "A" string on his Höfner violin bass. John's guitar picked up the sound from his amplifier, and the result was the first intentional use of guitar feedback in recorded music.[12] This mesmerizing ambient moan kicks off the hit "I Feel Fine." Guitar feedback quickly became a pillar of rock and roll and remains so to this day. In this section, we will look to harness the wisdom of Lennon and McCartney. How can we *intentionally* leverage the power of feedback?

Feedback is the second of the Five Thrive Factors, the primary contributing elements to teacher self-efficacy. Feedback describes providing information to teachers about their practice that can then inform future practice. Feedback directly bolsters self-reflection, the previous contributor of self-efficacy we explored, by offering content on which teachers can reflect.

Three characteristics of effective feedback emerged from this research. Effective feedback is thought-provoking, specific, and reciprocal. Any one of these characteristics will surely enhance the impact of feedback. When all three characteristics are abundantly present, we significantly increase the likelihood that the feedback will lead to improved instructional practices and, ultimately, improved student learning.

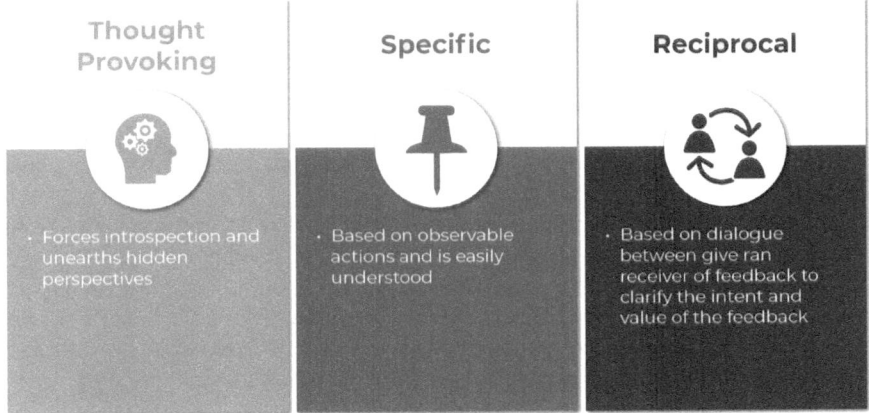

Characteristics of Effective Teacher Feedback. David Grambow, Applying the RTI Equation, 2021.

Thought-Provoking Feedback: Effective feedback provokes reflection, thought, and, ultimately, action. Once the feedback is provided, the receiver should be inspired to reflect on what was shared and integrate it with their self-perceptions and previously acquired feedback. One of the most effective ways to offer thought-provoking questions is to ask well-crafted open-ended questions.

Thought-provoking feedback can prompt the receiver to assimilate the new information with other sources of evidence, including their schema and past experiences. For instance, an instructional coach might share feedback by asking the teacher why she asked students a particular question at a particular point in the lesson. As the teacher is considering the thought-provoking prompt from the coach, she would likely be thinking of other instances when she used similar questioning techniques. The feedback serves as a way to connect past and current practice. Ideally, the coach would then follow up with questions about qualities that characterize effective questioning.

Thought-provoking feedback can inspire action by illuminating an undiscovered opportunity. For example, a principal might offer feedback to teachers that certain creative support offered to one student was remarkably successful and then follow up with a question about why the teacher thought it was so effective. This simple act of offering this feedback could inspire the teacher to systematize the practice so more students can benefit.

Finally, thought-provoking feedback encourages reflection. Feedback is essentially meaningless if the receiver does not internalize the feedback through reflection. This does not mean that all feedback must be accepted at face value. The reflection on the feedback often includes dismissing some of the elements as irrelevant while deciding which elements are worthy of consideration.

Specific Feedback: Effective feedback is laser-focused. This specificity helps the feedback receiver grasp the context of the feedback and the action that should be continued, discontinued, or adjusted. Specific feedback also allows for a call to action. Finally, feedback that points to specific action helps teachers generate a cognitive connection between their instructional choices. It helps take the subconscious to the conscious. So often choices are made at the subconscious level, resulting in choices and actions others can see, but we remain blind. Effective feedback illuminates those actions hidden from the power of self-reflection and allows teachers to capitalize on the perspectives of others.

Reciprocal Feedback: Effective feedback is reciprocal. Reciprocal feedback forms a relationship between the giver and receiver, allowing feedback to flow in both directions. A great example of reciprocal feedback that can have a positive impact is deliberately seeking feedback from students. For example, a teacher could confer with students to share feedback about student writing and at the same time ask the students to provide feedback about their teaching. This communicates to the student that their learning is a shared responsibility.

Reciprocal feedback can also occur between adults and is often realized by simply asking clarifying questions about received feedback. These clarifying questions can open lines of communication, allowing us to dig deeper for a more meaningful collaborative exploration of the teaching and learning process. Of the three elements of effective teacher feedback, reciprocity is the most challenging.

FEEDBACK: APPLICATION TO PRACTICE

Now that we have explored the theoretical qualities of effective feedback, we can look at the three practical forms in which feedback for teachers can come. These include encouraging feedback, critical feedback, and data-based feedback.

Effective Teacher Feedback Framework

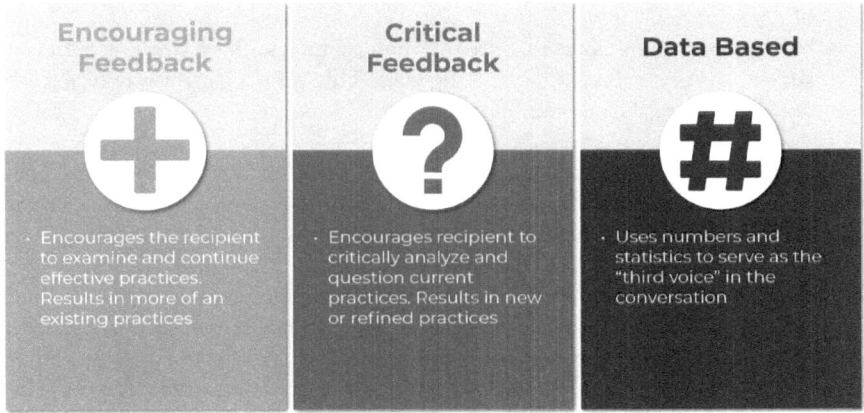

Effective Teacher Feedback Framework. David Grambow, Effective Teacher Feedback Framework, 2021.

Encouraging Feedback: Encouraging feedback is designed to have the recipient continue effective practices. It reinforces teachers to continue to persevere through challenges. Encouraging feedback is highly effective for teachers who are naturally skilled but not necessarily technicians. Encouraging feedback is the easiest to receive. Therefore, it may serve as the entrée to the world of effectively receiving feedback, which is a skill in and of itself.

The provider of encouraging feedback can help teachers realize the "why" behind a practice. For instance, a teacher may be naturally skilled at making personal connections with students. A coach could offer the following feedback: "You consistently make a point to make personal connections with your kids. This helps develop trusting relationships that will encourage your students to take risks." This feedback encourages the teacher to continue the practice while developing pedagogical knowledge of why it is effective.

Some examples of encouraging feedback include:

- "When you asked your students about the factors contributing to the American Revolution, their conversation made it clear that you have been encouraging them to consider multiple perspectives. Keep doing that!"
- "One of your colleagues recognized you as being especially helpful as you worked through your curriculum review. I appreciate how you go out of your way to be a wonderful teammate."

- "As a special educator, you play an important role in creating inclusive environments. Your co-teaching in this school has been transformational. I especially appreciate the way you explain the 'why' behind the choices you make on behalf of our students."
- "I was walking by your hall this morning, and I noticed you greeted every student as they walked into your trig class. This is such a great way to foster a positive culture. Thank you!"

You may have noticed a pattern with these examples of encouraging feedback. They address all three elements of effective feedback. First, they open with an observation that provides context and specificity. Second, they follow why the observed behavior is worthy of repetition that is thought-provoking and specific. Finally, it closes with a heartfelt recognition. This personal touch invites a reciprocal conversation.

Critical Feedback: In contrast to the encouraging style, some feedback can be critical. Critical feedback is focused on the art of reconsideration. By providing feedback on some aspects of the teaching and learning process that may benefit from reconsideration, we open the doors to a complete feedback system. Critical feedback complements encouraging feedback. When skillfully provided and received, critical feedback can offer transformational insight.

Critical does not necessarily mean negative. Take, for instance, a film critic. Their role is not to tear down every movie they see with reckless abandon. Instead, their role is to allow others to benefit from their trained eye and expertise. We should always think about critical feedback from the most positive perspective and with a growth mindset. If we apply a critical eye to practices we believe provide the most significant opportunity for growth, we empower our colleagues to maximize their self-efficacy. This can be a rewarding experience for both the giver and receiver of the critical feedback if done with finesse.

Critical feedback is constructive for those who are most open to feedback. If teachers are not skilled in the art of receiving feedback, or if they are insecure in their practice, critical feedback can, at best, be ignored, or, at worst, negatively impact the teacher. Starting small and strategically when venturing into the realm of critical feedback can help forge a path toward success. Consider it a BIG win if we can move from resistance to acceptance of critical feedback, as it surely will open opportunities for transformational growth.

Some examples of critical feedback include:

- "I noticed over one-half of your students did not offer any input during your lesson. How could you increase the engagement of all students?"
- "Your growth report indicates a decrease in the number of students meeting their growth target. What do you think might be contributing to that?"
- "How do you feel about your ability to reach students with special needs?" (Open-ended questions like this could be used as critical feedback if there is an issue related to the question.)

- "You might try asking more open-ended questions to encourage higher-order thinking."
- "I noticed quite a bit of 'teacher talk' and not a lot of 'student talk.' You could work with a coach to track the ratio and see if you could increase student engagement in your lessons."

Data-Based Feedback: Some feedback is steeped in complex data. Data-based feedback allows teachers who rely on quantifiable and measurable guidance to enjoy the power of feedback. When engaging in data-based feedback, we allow data to serve as the third voice in the dialogue surrounding teaching behavior and the subsequent student results. For the record, data-based feedback can be encouraging or critical, depending on the nature of the data.

For some context, here are some simple examples of data-based feedback:

- You spent 12 minutes speaking, and your students spent 16 minutes speaking during the observation.
- 62% of your students met their growth target on the most recent interim assessment.
- Your students of color represent 45% of your office referrals and represent 20% of your total student population.

Notice that in these examples, the feedback includes no judgment, just facts. This sort of feedback is beneficial for those who gravitate toward the quantifiable or those who are resistant to the perspective of others. As they say, you can't argue with the facts. These three styles of feedback do not need to exist in isolation. The art of offering effective feedback lies in our ability to include the three characteristics of effective feedback as much as possible and to know when to choose which of the three forms of feedback. In the next section, we will explore how you can seek feedback that can unleash your efficacy.

HOW TO EFFECTIVELY RECEIVE FEEDBACK

For teachers who crave feedback, it may be difficult to understand why some others do not take advantage of the power of feedback as a means to improve their instruction. Accepting feedback is not a natural skill for everyone. Like any skill, it can be practiced, and everyone can improve. Feedback is now ubiquitously accepted as a means to improve teaching and is embedded in coaching, evaluation, and collaboration. We can more deeply understand the potential aversion to feedback by exploring the evolution of the word's meaning.

The term *feedback* originates from the world of industry and technology. It entered the common lexicon when feedback described the process of audio output being reintroduced into the system as input creating a loop. This loop creates a dissonant squeal that increases indefinitely until the input is removed. Not everyone feels fine when they receive feedback. Remember the Beatles and their hit "I Feel Fine?" The Beatles created a sound that, up until that point, would have been scrubbed from any professional recording. The Beatles, however, deliberately kept the feedback in the recording. Like the Beatles, teachers must be intentional and poised to accept the feedback to fully capitalize on it. We must not receive it as a jarring imposition.

When someone offers feedback, they offer their perspective. The receiver of the feedback must decide what to do with that feedback. They have several choices. They can deny the feedback, assuming it is a faulty perspective. They can assimilate the feedback with their existing schema and allow it to influence their future decisions indirectly. They can also fully embrace the feedback and take immediate and direct action. There is no correct answer.

We have all experienced the sensation of becoming defensive when we receive feedback. What was it about that feedback that made you feel defensive? For some, it is that the feedback felt overly judgmental. For others, it is that the feedback seemed overgeneralized based on limited observation of the particular context of the feedback. Sometimes, it is quite simply that the feedback receiver did not respect the opinion of the individual offering feedback.

How do we get to the point where we can openly accept the feedback and "feel fine" without a defensive response? Douglas Stone and Sheila Heen offer some practical wisdom related to effectively receiving feedback in their book, *Thanks for the Feedback: The Science and Art of Receiving Feedback Well*. They suggest that controlling emotions plays the most important role in accepting critical feedback.[13]

They also suggest clarifying the intention of the person who is offering the feedback. This directly aligns with the concept of reciprocal feedback by creating an opportunity for a feedback loop. In other words, how can we help ourselves effectively receive feedback while returning feedback about the process to increase the other person's ability to offer constructive feedback in the future? Stone and Heen point out that sometimes our emotional response to feedback is more related to the "who" than the "what."[14] If the relationship with the person offering the feedback is not based on mutual trust and respect, it may be hard to receive it. Do your best to separate the message from the messenger. Focus on how you can grow from the feedback.

It is critical to get in touch with your emotions and analyze your response with as much vigor as you analyze the feedback. Do not let your imagination take over and take you down the rabbit hole of overanalyzing the feedback. Instead, take it for what it is and move on. What it all boils down to is this: only pay attention to the feedback if it helps you improve. The following questions will help you apply our theory and framework to understand better how you currently grow from the feedback and your potential next steps.

FEEDBACK: REFLECTION QUESTIONS

The power of self-reflection is highlighted throughout this book. Consider the following reflective questions about the story of Jaime Escalante and the power of feedback:

- How would you describe the relationship between ganas (desire) and creencia (belief)?
- How realistic would it be to teach like Mr. Escalante in your school setting? Why?
- Which style(s) of feedback do you prefer (encouraging, critical, data based)?
- How could you improve the way you currently capitalize on feedback?
- How can you help your colleagues by deliberately offering feedback aligned with what we have learned?

FEEDBACK THRIVE CHALLENGE

Write an elevator speech between three to five sentences describing the kind of feedback you value. Share this elevator speech with someone who regularly provides you feedback and ask them what they value in feedback.

THE HABIT OF COLLABORATION: COLLABORATION ACTIVATORS

So what is collaboration anyway? At its simplest level, collaboration is two or more people working together toward a shared goal. However, collaboration is more than work. Collaboration allows team members to be part of something larger than themselves. When teams strategically collaborate, they amplify their individual talents and skills. Collaboration harnesses the power of synergy and allows teams to do so much more than the sum total of their individual contributions.

- Think of the most rewarding professional collaborative effort of which you have been a part. What made it rewarding?
- Think of a time when you found a professional collaborative effort frustrating. What made it frustrating?
- What makes you a good collaborator?
- What skills could you refine to improve your collaborative capacity?

COLLABORATION VIGNETTE: LEARNING SUPPORT SERVICES

Collaboration is a crucial driver of teacher self-efficacy. Sometimes collaboration occurs within small, informal groups. Collaboration can also be fostered through structural changes at the district level. The following vignette is the story of collaboration that was made possible by reimagining the student support structures. Many traditional school structures are based on systems that are "collaborative in name only." Restructuring of systems can lead to transformative collaborative opportunities if it is designed intentionally and is supported systemically.

One district took this challenge seriously and decided to restructure their departments to meet the needs of their students more collaboratively. As a district leadership team, they recognized that their siloed approach to supporting all students exacerbated inequities. So the superintendent asked a simple question: "How can we restructure our district team to match our desired outcomes?" Their first step was combining their Curriculum and Instruction department and their Student Services department into one overarching department they named Learning Support Services. This allowed collaborative decision-making regarding core curriculum, intervention, special education, gifted and talented programming, and social-emotional learning.

They faced a cultural challenge familiar to many similar districts. This district was an affluent suburban district with very little diversity. Affluent communities can fall into the trap of masking inequities. The masking of inequities can be intentional or unintentional. This district fell into the trap of masking inequities with overly generalized strong academic achievement results. It was easy for them to rest on their laurels with high graduation rates, higher than average ACT scores, and impressive Advanced Placement results. These results, however, masked inequities existing throughout their district, including achievement gaps, lagging inclusive practices, and learned helplessness.

They found this challenge well-suited for their Learning Support Services team. They quickly identified Response to Intervention (RtI) as a limiting structure. The basic premise of RtI is fundamentally solid. It is essentially a tiered approach to identifying and supporting struggling learners. It is intended to allow for early intervention while measuring the effectiveness of the interventions. They adopted an RtI approach to identifying students with disabilities. This logical approach inadvertently generated challenges.

RtI limited students and their teachers in several ways. Too often, decision-makers were viewing RtI as the path to special education. In an RtI-based learning disability eligibility system, a school must document the use of qualifying interventions. As a result, teams were subconsciously seeking interventions that "counted" as a stepping-stone toward special education.

The Learning Support Services team completely restructured their RtI system and ensured all decisions were made with all students in mind from the start. They created collaborative work teams to redesign their student interventions to become more inclusive, close the achievement gap for students of color, and scale up their co-teaching opportunities. They were developing collective efficacy. Collective efficacy is the belief a learning community has in its skills and abilities to positively impact student achievement. This is precisely how the Learning Support Services team was thriving.

TEACHER-FOCUSED VERSUS STUDENT-FOCUSED COLLABORATION

You can categorize collaboration in an instructional environment as either teacher-focused or student-focused. Although these two forms of collaboration may look very similar to the teachers engaged in the collaborative effort, they will feel significantly different to an outside observer. The outside observer may not register the distinction because the work product may be very similar while the underlying goal of the collaboration varies.

Professionals engaged in teacher-focused collaboration spend their energies on adult practices and decisions. For example, a team of teachers may decide to engage in a book talk about best-practice math instruction out of a desire to learn more. This laudable collaborative effort is symbolic of a high degree of professionalism. We could assume students will benefit from their professional learning, but their goal is to increase their professional knowledge.

Teachers who engage in student-focused collaboration concern themselves with student outcomes. Take the same group of math teachers, but consider it from a different perspective. Imagine this group of teachers recognizing that a sizable portion of their students lack the necessary algebraic reasoning to meet course objectives independently. As a result, they collaboratively generate outcome goals for their students and identify a relevant book to study to build their skills.

This may look exactly the same to a passerby, but the focus is entirely different. While both forms of collaboration are beneficial and support teacher self-efficacy, student-focused collaboration tends to be more impactful. This enhanced impact is generated from the inherent feedback loop created when these collaborative teachers focus on student outcomes to see progress toward the goals they have created. In addition, students are more likely to reap the benefits of their collaboration, which also supports self-efficacy.

COLLABORATION: REFLECTION QUESTIONS AND CHALLENGES

- How would your close colleagues describe your collaboration skills?
- How would your supervisor describe your collaboration skills?
- How would you describe the kind of colleague with whom you most enjoy collaborating?
- What was the most impactful collaboration you have ever engaged in?
- How did that collaboration impact your students?

COLLABORATION THRIVE CHALLENGE

Make a list of every team with whom you regularly collaborate. Discuss the concept of teacher-focused versus student-focused collaboration. As a group, pick one aspect of your collaborative endeavors that could be more student-focused. Develop a plan including goal setting for students that would make it more collaborative. After two or three team meetings about the identified goals, discuss how the switch to student-focused collaboration impacted your team and your students.

4

Focus of Thriving Teachers

The final two Thrive Factors that contribute to the self-efficacy of teachers describe the focus of thriving teachers. By explicitly focusing professional energies in the right direction, teachers naturally support their self-efficacy. Focus requires energy, and energy is a finite resource. Teachers who thrive are judicious when it comes to spending this resource. If handled well, spending energy focusing in the right direction serves as an investment in self-efficacy.

Teachers often describe focusing an inordinate amount of time on managing student behavior as a stressor. However, when we dig a little deeper, we realize that this reactive response focused on managing behaviors depletes energy and erodes self-efficacy. The two areas of focus we will explore, student relationships and inclusion, can proactively support positive student behavior. As teachers maintain this focus and hone their skills, they bolster their self-efficacy and improve the learning experience for their students.

Teachers also point to increasing expectations for academic achievement as a stressful challenge and a potential mitigator of their self-efficacy. The focus factors of relationships and inclusion support increased levels of student achievement, thus limiting the stress related to increased expectations and subsequently increasing teacher self-efficacy. With strong relationships, teachers can supportively expect more of their students. Their focus on inclusion helps them build the specific skills to meet the needs of a classroom with a broader range of academic needs.

Thriving teachers focus on developing strong and meaningful student relationships. As you will learn, focusing on student relationships builds trust, increases engagement, and ultimately allows teachers to strengthen their student engagement and classroom community-building self-efficacy.

Thriving teachers also focus on inclusion. Teachers naturally build their self-efficacy by focusing on increasing inclusion by learning and applying strategies to meet more diverse populations of students. When teachers learn that these strategies work, they bolster their beliefs and want to try more. Teachers who feel efficacious in a highly inclusive teaching environment are likely operating at peak efficacy levels. When combined with the three habits of thriving teachers, these two areas of focus open doors and break down barriers for teachers and their students.

STUDENT RELATIONSHIP ACTIVATORS

In the following vignette, you will learn a counternarrative to the Hollywood perspective of what excellent teaching is all about. You will read about Angie Scioli, the subject of the documentary *Teacher of the Year*.[1]

- What does it take to earn a "Teacher of the Year" award?
- Would you like to be recognized as Teacher of the Year? Why or why not?
- Would you feel the same if your students' test scores were included in the determination of the award recipient?
- When your students do not perform as well as you would have liked on a high-stakes assessment, how do you feel?
- How might you analyze student results to guarantee a self-efficacy increasing experience?

STUDENT RELATIONSHIP VIGNETTE: ANGIE SCIOLI—TEACHER OF THE YEAR

Earlier, we explored Jaime Escalante and the film *Stand and Deliver*. Critics have often questioned the value and veracity of sensationalized Hollywood films such as this about teacher underdogs defying the odds and achieving monumental success with marginalized students. Although I am a self-admitted consumer and fan of these inspirational films, I understand the criticism. So do Rob Phillips and Jay Korreck, the filmmakers behind the documentary *Teacher of the Year*, which explores the challenges and successes of Angie Scioli, a real teacher facing the challenges all teachers do.

Hollywood productions, due to economic necessity, must dramatize their stories to boost box-office returns. One way they dramatize these stories is by creating "David and Goliath" narratives. Unfortunately, a story about an amazingly dedicated teacher who sacrifices time with her family, politically advocates for the profession, and gives so much of herself on a daily basis in suburban North Carolina just does not make for a Hollywood blockbuster. It certainly does, however, make for a compelling documentary.

Teacher of the Year sets out to dispel the savior myth Hollywood often portrays while shining light on an actual day-to-day grind of dedicated teaching. This story begins on a sunny Saturday morning in suburban North Carolina. Angie Scioli is in her kitchen, lovingly making chocolate-chip pancakes for her two energetic and curious daughters and her devoted husband . . . and her former high school students. Scioli's inspiring but painfully realistic story is one of equal parts dedication and exhaustion. Scioli certainly enjoys high levels of teacher self-efficacy. Her students will undoubtedly tell you she is a thriving teacher.

Scioli is, however, not immune to feeling ignored, underappreciated, and undersupported. At one point in her career, she almost threw in the towel and decided to step off the gas pedal and just get by. "What kind of idiot works tirelessly for twenty years, stressing out each day to make every lesson the best it can be, worrying about scores of kids when what I do is not valued by the people in power?" Scioli asked herself. Nevertheless, her students and her dedication to the profession provided the wind in her sails she needed to keep going.

Scioli excelled as a teacher of social studies at Leesville Road High School in Raleigh, North Carolina. Scioli built authentic and enduring relationships with her students. Her students shared their perspectives about the positive impact she has had on their lives. If you walked by her classroom, it would not be out of the ordinary to find Scioli garbed in an elaborate costume of a pertinent historical figure. Another example of her commitment to building relationships with her students is her Saturday morning pancake breakfast tradition. This tradition included former students coming to her house to talk about life in their twenties, while enjoying homemade pancakes with their former high school teacher.

At one point in the film, Angie's self-efficacy is brutally challenged when she finds the standardized testing results of her students indicate that she is, according to the mandated teacher evaluation system, "ineffective." Why is this the case? With all Scioli does for her students, why do some students still not excel according to these standardized test scores? Because this is real life. Because there are variables at play that are not easily measured on a standardized test, including political forces.

Angie not only continues to dedicate herself to her students but she also founded a political movement to shine a light on the underfunded and ignored North Carolina public education system. She awoke from what she referred to as her "privileged oblivion" to realize the larger political and economic systems that require reform and a serious commitment to children. She not only wanted to thrive in her classroom and have her students thrive, she also set her sights on supporting every teacher in her state. This dedication does not happen without a high level of teacher self-efficacy.

Angie's talent and dedication to building meaningful relationships benefited her students, but, equally important, they fueled her self-efficacy. One can simply watch a few of Angie's YouTube lectures to behold her dedication to her students and craft. In 2020, Scioli's YouTube presence took on a more significant meaning as she, along with every teacher across the country, wrestled with the best way to provide instruction during a pandemic.

It is heartwarming to watch Angie's interactive YouTube lessons delivered during the COVID-19 crisis. She begins the lessons by greeting the students, asking about their lives, and sharing about hers. Angie's focus on students illustrates the beautiful reciprocal nature of enriching relationships. Life is hard. Teaching is hard. By building relationships like Angie does, we collectively bolster our ability to face each day, knowing we can make a difference.

STUDENT RELATIONSHIP THEORY: THE THREE DIMENSIONS OF EDUCATIONAL CARE

Educational care theory suggests teachers provide care for their students across three dimensions.[2] The three dimensions include personal care, pedagogical care, and interpersonal care. As is the case with many of the theories we explore, Schat's model suggests that these dimensions work interdependently. Certainly, teachers may demonstrate a stronger proclivity toward one dimension, but in the most caring environments, all dimensions are addressed. Teachers with the most robust and meaningful relationships nurture all three dimensions with their students.

The personal care dimension describes the individual personal relationships teachers develop with their students as individuals. This is the dimension of care that most people think about when they picture a caring teacher. Teachers manifest this dimension by focusing on each student with specific needs and interests and expressing care for each student. Although there is no predetermined order in which teachers develop or communicate each dimension of care, personal care is certainly foundational from the student perspective. It may be challenging for a student to recognize care expressed in the other dimensions if they feel their teacher does not care about them as an individual.

The pedagogical dimension describes the way teachers care for their students as learners. Outside observers may perceive this dimension of care very differently than they would personal care. Pedagogical care is communicated by genuine care for the academic development of each student. Pedagogical care is a cornerstone in a personalized learning environment. Teachers expressing this dimension understand their responsibility to engage all students in the learning process individually based on their unique needs.

Finally, the interpersonal dimension addresses classroom culture issues and describes how teachers care for their students as part of the community. This is the most complex of the three dimensions as it involves multiple stakeholders. Each of the three dimensions is made up of several elements. There are eight intertwined elements in the interpersonal dimensions compared to only three in each of the other dimensions. In addition, it involves such complex constructs as culture and power dynamics. As we will explore in more detail in subsequent chapters, many teachers struggle with this dimension despite their authentic care and concern for each student.

The power of Schat's model lies in its synthesis of existing theory. Many consistent elements of educational care have been identified. Schat identified the three dimensions under which many elements exist. Schat also recognized a dimension that was largely missing from the existing body of research. He identified the interpersonal dimension stressing the importance of classroom culture in fostering a caring environment. He found "if a teacher did not ensure that each student was a safe and valued member of a learning community, the students would not experience educational care, regardless of the teacher's caring intentions."[3]

Three Dimensions of Educational Care

Personal	Pedagogical	Interpersonal
The teacher cares for each student As a person	The teacher cares for each student As a learner	The teacher cares for each student As a member of the classroom community

Three Dimensions of Educational Care. Sean Schat. Element of Educational Care, "Exploring Care in Education." *International Christian Community of Teacher Educators Journal* 13(2): 1–10 (2018).[4]

STUDENT RELATIONSHIP: APPLICATION TO PRACTICE

We have explored the fantastic relationship-building skills of Angie Scioli and learned a bit about a theory that explains various aspects of strong relationships with students. We will now turn our attention to operationalizing student relationships to support self-efficacy development. There are three avenues you can explore to boost your self-efficacy. They include leveraging the relationship for academic success, focusing on relationships beyond academics, and building classroom community.

Leveraging Relationships for Academic Success

Facilitating academic success is the most direct route to enhancing your self-efficacy through your strong relationships with students. By developing authentic relationships with your students, you can push a little harder, expect a little more, and dig deeper. Unfortunately, we have all witnessed teachers who develop great relationships with students but do not leverage those relationships for student growth. Conversely, we have all witnessed teachers who can push students so unabatedly it makes us uncomfortable yet the student ends up feeling empowered. This is a teacher who knows how to leverage student relationships for academic success.

When you leverage relationships for academic success, you are tapping into the pedagogical dimension of care. How do we develop the capacity to lean into our relationship strengths to support our students' academic growth? The first step is to be deliberate. If we do not intentionally analyze the strength of our relationships with students and then decide how we will leverage the relationships, we are unlikely to maximize the impact. For instance, you may naturally develop strong relationships with students. It is likely, however, that the rate at which those relationships develop varies wildly. This would suggest that your ability to leverage the relationships to challenge students academically should vary in equal measure. To capitalize on these opportunities for individual students, you must analyze the strength of the relationships and act both deliberately and systematically.

However, we cannot overestimate the depth of each relationship and assume because a student laughs at our teacher jokes, they are ready to be challenged as much as they may be after the relationships are guaranteed and solid. I encourage you to consider the depth and authenticity of your relationships using the Dimensions of Care Theory previously discussed. The following questions can help you gauge the strength of your relationships:

- What do I know about each of my students?
- What do my students know about the real me?
- How often do my students seek guidance for academic support?
- How can I be certain my students know I care about them as individuals?
- How would I describe my classroom community?
- How do my students support one another through authentic caring relationships?

Now we will turn our attention to the important aspects of vibrant teacher-student relationships focused beyond the realm of academics.

Focusing on Relationships that Transcend Academics

Teachers who focus on relationships that transcend academics engage in a fascinating dynamic. The vast majority of teachers cite their desire to build meaningful relationships with students as a prime motivator for pursuing a career in education. However, when we dig a little deeper, we find these teachers typically describe the nature of the relationship outside the realm of academics. The reality of the job sets in for most teachers early in their careers, and they come to realize the pressure to get results. As a result, their focus begins to shift more to academics. To reap the self-efficacy-enhancing benefits of relationship building, we need to revisit one of the cornerstones of self-efficacy theory—self-efficacy is context-specific.

The fact that self-efficacy is context-specific simply means that there is no universal construct of teacher self-efficacy. Teachers may feel quite efficacious instructionally yet lack self-efficacy when it comes to student engagement. Think back to the revised model for teacher self-efficacy, which includes four domains: instructional self-efficacy, engagement self-efficacy, classroom community self-efficacy, and self-care efficacy. Student relationships beyond academics directly fuel the engagement self-efficacy as well as the classroom community self-efficacy domains.

Consider, for instance, a student with whom you feel you have a strong personal relationship. The personal connections you share with this student likely bolster your belief in your ability to engage this student. Extending this idea, if you develop strong personal relationships with your students, you will likely enhance your self-efficacy related to student engagement with the bonus of building classroom community.

Here are some quick tips for building relationships to help give your self-efficacy a boost:

1. *Systematically learn your students' names as quickly as possible.* This helps your students feel seen and heard. In addition, it lets them know you see them as individual people.
2. *Use the names.* Calling students by name frequently builds relationships. Unfortunately, it is all too easy to fall into a pattern where we stop using names. Pay attention to this one. You might be surprised how infrequently a student hears their name.
3. *Share personal stories.* Slide the curtain back a bit, and you will be surprised how much more relatable you become. By giving your student a peek into the other aspects of your life, you create a personal bond. It also helps dispel the myth that you live in your classroom. Of course, professional boundaries are important, but staying connected on a human level is critical.
4. *Do not live in your classroom!* You need to take care of yourself. By doing so, you will develop great stories to share with your students, and you will feel more refreshed and able to focus on the social-emotional needs of your students. It is not helpful to anyone, most importantly you and your students, to work so hard that you become exhausted and stressed.
5. *Ask questions.* By simply asking questions, you demonstrate genuine care for your students. Of course, not all students want to engage in these types of conversations. Sometimes quiet questions when no one else is listening feel safer.
6. *Reflect.* This, of course, recalls a previous factor that contributes to self-efficacy. Reflect on relationships by thinking about the students you have not recently shared a personal connection with and deliberately act on that knowledge.
7. *Attend outside activities.* Nothing speaks more profoundly to your care of a student than showing up to an outside activity. This certainly helps build relationships with families too! A word of caution—not all kids engage in traditional outside activities. You will want to be cautious about inadvertently exacerbating inequities by providing more attention to particular students.

8. *Finally, just be yourself.* You are a professional educator. You chose this career because you care. Just being yourself will allow authentic and meaningful relationships to blossom, and you do not even need to try!

By building strong relationships with students that extend beyond the realm of academics, you naturally strengthen the cultural fabric in your classroom. Your students feel cared for, your engagement self-efficacy and classroom-community self-efficacy are enhanced, and everyone learns more! Consider the following questions to gauge your proclivity toward enhancing your self-efficacy by focusing on student relationships:

- How do you go about building relationships with your students?
- What is the last personal connection you remember making with a student?
- How do you engage students who resist engagement?
- How does it feel when you connect with a student who resists personal connection?
- Who is a teacher you had with whom you had a strong relationship?
- Describe your level of engagement with that teacher compared to a teacher with whom your relationship was not as strong.
- What can you do tomorrow to build a stronger relationship with one student?

Building Classroom Community

Strong classroom communities are characterized by student investment in the culture of the classroom. By focusing on classroom communities, teachers expand their focus from their relationship with each individual student to their relationship with the class and the relationships among the students. Building classroom community is not a more advanced form of focusing on student relationships. It is a complementary addition to the many ways strong student relationships support self-efficacy.

The four pillars of classroom community include democratic decision-making, co-created rules and norms, student voice in the learning, and supported relationships. Students who have a say in how the class operates tend to engage more meaningfully in the learning process. Teachers must deliberately focus on the development and support of the classroom community. These four pillars work in conjunction to form the supportive fabric of a strong classroom community that empowers students and improves equitable outcomes.

Democratic Decision-Making

By focusing on student interpersonal and intrapersonal relationships to build classroom community, you empower yourself and your students. Strong classroom communities support democratic decision-making. This does not mean that all decisions are made by bringing all issues to the students for a vote. Democratic decision-

The 4 Pillars of Classroom Community

Democratic Decision Making	Co-Created Rules and Norms	Student Voice in Learning	Supported Relationships
Students are included in decision making when possible. The parameters for student involvement are clearly understood by all stakeholders.	Student and teachers work together to create rule for the class and norms for groups. These rules and norms are based on the interests and goals of the students.	Students are provided opportunities for meaningful voice in the teaching and learning process. Teachers actively seek input and feedback from the students.	Relationships among students and adults are intentionally supported and fostered. There are specific procedures to rebuild relationship when conflict arises.

The Four Pillars of Classroom Community. David Grambow. *The Four Pillars of Classroom Community*. 2021.

making in a classroom community simply means students are intentionally included in shared decision-making deliberately and when developmentally appropriate.

Teachers support democratic decision-making in their classrooms by intentionally engaging students in shared decision-making where the parameters for student involvement are clearly understood. Democratic decision-making increases student engagement and teacher engagement efficacy. In addition, students in such a classroom community are likely to accept the collective responsibility for their success and the success of their classmates.

Fostering classroom community through democratic decision-making supports not only teachers' self-efficacy but also serves as one of the most impactful strategies for supporting student self-efficacy. Democratic decision-making contributes to the overall classroom community by creating a forum where students' ideas, goals, and contributions are valued. Students learn how to advocate for themselves and their classmates, thus increasing their sense of efficacy.

Co-Created Rules and Norms

Strong classroom communities require collaboratively developed systems that support interpersonal relationships. Clear expectations that are developed *with* students, not *for* students, strengthen the classroom community by increasing student investment in the process and outcomes. Furthermore, these rules and expectations should be reinforced *with* students, not imposed *upon* students.

Co-creating rules and expectations builds student and teacher agency. Agency is an empowering concept that describes how we all make choices impacting our world and the world around us. When we increase student agency by allowing them to take an active role in developing classroom expectations, we tell them that their voice matters and that the classroom is a place designed by them and for them. Albert Bandura has consistently described the inherent connection between human agency and self-efficacy. Essentially, by acting with agency and taking control over our environment, we can develop self-efficacy. By inviting students into a process that traditionally has been very autocratic, we are fostering student agency. The impact of this invitation for your students to participate in the development of expectations is amplified as it contributes to your self-efficacy.

There is considerable debate around the semantics of student expectations. For the sake of simplicity, we will look at "rules" as the general guidelines that reinforce the expectations for students and teachers and address issues such as safety and order. Norms, however, describe the way students want to treat others and be treated. Typically, you will have one set of rules but a variety of norms for different classroom functions such as group work, presentations, and independent or choice-based activities. They are both critical elements to a robust student-centered classroom community. Peruse these few guidelines for co-creating rules and norms:

1. *Start with the students' hopes, dreams, and goals.* This may seem a bit elementary, but a developmentally appropriate approach to creating expectations that support the actual desires of students is critical and should take place within the first few days in any new classroom environment.
2. *Be authentic.* Certainly, we could expect that the big categories of respect, safety, and responsibility will emerge; leave space for norms and rules that truly reflect the culture of your students.
3. *Do not be afraid to include nonnegotiables.* There is undoubtedly a place for teacher voice in this process. If there is a necessary, student-centered guideline that is not coming to light from the students, by all means, introduce it into the conversation. This process should not strip you of your agency.
4. *Ritualize the process.* The establishment of rules and norms plays such a critical role in developing a highly functioning classroom community that ritualizing the process increases the gravitas. You could accomplish this ritualization by having each student formally share their goals for the rest of the class to celebrate.

This process of co-creation of rules is a way to significantly include student voice in the management side of classroom community. Student voice in the learning process is also a critical element of the classroom community-building process.

Student Voice in Learning

Building relationships to strengthen classroom community significantly contributes to teacher self-efficacy. This sort of relationship-building supports classroom community efficacy and student engagement efficacy. It also, however, directly supports instructional self-efficacy if we focus on the inclusion of student voice in the teaching and learning process. By maintaining a focus on building your classroom community to deliberately include student voice in teaching and learning, you can create a truly dynamic and student-centered classroom community. Here are six ways to encourage more student voice in the learning process:

1. *Increase personal relevance for students.* Leverage the diversity in your classroom by finding ways to connect your intended learning outcomes to the fundamental interests of your students. If you are not sure what those interests are, just ask!
2. *Allow for open-ended discussion.* Open-ended discussion encourages student voice by clearly communicating that you, as the teacher, do not have all the answers. Open-ended questioning techniques, of course, foster higher-order thinking for students as well. By loosening the reins a bit, students can express themselves and strengthen the fabric of the classroom community.
3. *Encourage creativity.* By allowing students to represent their learning creatively, you are letting your students tap into their talents and interests that may be hidden in a one-size-fits-all representation of learning. Just be clear with parameters, so students understand their responsibilities. Co-creating rubrics creates abundant opportunities to accomplish this goal.
4. *Amplify marginalized voices.* Strong classroom communities hold the transformative potential of amplifying voices that may be silenced in a traditional power structure. Be deliberate and courageous as you work to bring those silenced voices to the forefront. All students will be the better for it, and your self-efficacy will surely be enhanced.
5. *Be open to differences of opinion.* Respectful debate is a lost art that we can revitalize by encouraging honest discussions of differences of opinions among our students. This can be a bit scary as you give up a lot of control, and the conversation could veer away from your district's curriculum. Clarity of expectations is the name of the game.
6. *Use norms, rubrics, and protocols.* We have discussed norms previously. Lean into using these specific sets of norms for any activity where you are trying to amplify student agency and voice. Co-creating rubrics with students to spell out expectations empowers students and ensures learning outcomes align with expectations. Protocols provide structure for democratic adult or student conversations.

Supported Relationships

Conflict is inevitable in any human endeavor. The risk for conflict is exacerbated when teachers strive for more student voices in decision-making. This is a risk well worth taking. It would, of course, be easier to run an autocratic teacher-centric classroom, but it would not benefit teacher or student self-efficacy. Two guiding principles will help ensure student relationships are supported in a manner that enriches and strengthens classroom community. First, relationships must be supported proactively. Secondly, relationships must be supported responsively.

It is far easier to establish the foundation for strong relationships early on than it is to try to repair strained relationships. Teachers who proactively establish strong relationships among all students place themselves to maximize the potential of their classroom community. All of the other classroom community-building strategies we have discussed so far fall into the category of proactively developing relationships. However, in this section, we are interested in addressing conflict that threatens to damage relationships.

First, accept and plan for the inevitable conflicts that will arise. Embrace them. Conflict in itself is not destructive, nor does it necessarily damage relationships. By planning for resolving conflict proactively and transparently with your students, you can leverage conflict as a means to clarify intent and ultimately build more authentic relationships. Engage your students in conversations about ways they resolve conflict with their friends and glean the appropriate lessons from that conversation. Remember that this is a lifelong skill for your students and not simply an exercise in classroom management.

Whatever proactive strategies you put into dealing with inevitable conflict, including the following three principles, will help ensure success. First, focus on understanding perspective. Although the responsibility for conflict is rarely a 50/50 endeavor, it is rarely entirely the responsibility of one party. Regardless of perceived blame, understanding the perspectives of all stakeholders is critical. Developing an understanding of perspectives presents a wonderful opportunity for another protocol.

Second, don't turn a conflict into a crisis by assuming it must be dealt with immediately. If safety is not an immediate concern, giving students some time to cool off to more openly engage in dialogue is critical. By establishing spaces in the classroom or the school where students can take a break and collect their thoughts, you will more likely engage them in authentic problem-solving. It is crucially important that you know when your students are ready to cool off. Sometimes that cooling-off needs to be facilitated by a skilled teacher. You risk fanning the flames of conflict if you expect students to cool off when they are not ready.

Third, help students understand their emotional triggers by proactively planning for the big three of fear, frustration, and anxiety. Proactively helping your students understand that these three emotions are often at the heart of interpersonal and intrapersonal conflict can prevent some turmoil from arising or increase the effectiveness of the problem-solving process. If it turns out that fear, frustration, and anxiety are not the emotional underpinnings for the conflict, leave space to hear directly from the students about the emotion involved in the conflict.

As we have established, conflict happens. Sometimes we will need to respond. *Respond* is the operative word here. We do not want to react out of emotion. A reaction is instantaneous and often unintentional. A reaction can explode from your reptilian brain and circumvent all of the circuitry designed to elicit a more thoughtful and comprehensive approach. Reaction is programmed into our fight or flight defense mechanisms that can inadvertently make a conflict worse by exacerbating the emotions of fear, frustration, and anxiety.

Responsiveness is based on a planned and thoughtful response. Responsiveness can slow down the swirling emotions around conflict and help us get to the heart of the matter. Responsiveness emerges from a combination of the unconscious and conscious and can link back directly to our proactive plans for dealing with conflict. For instance, you may have developed a protocol about dealing with differences regarding group work expectations. By being responsive, we can cool emotions and recognize opportunities to use this protocol to de-escalate and rebuild relationships.

While working toward responsive conflict resolution, we must remember that conflict impacts the entire class, not just those directly involved. By being responsive, we can tap into all of the strategies and skills we have learned and engage other stakeholders when appropriate. This may take the form of a classroom meeting at the elementary level or a restorative circle at the secondary level. No matter the form, responsive conflict resolution doesn't just resolve conflict. Ultimately, it builds relationships and strengthens classroom community.

Certainly, the intertwining of the varied forms of student-teacher relationships, the dimension of care theory, and the four domains of teacher self-efficacy are complex. Do not let this intimidate you. It is quite simple when distilled to their essential components. By building strong and multidimensional relationships with students, we can enhance our self-efficacy in all domains. At the risk of sounding like a broken record, it is all about intentionality. Not unlike a relationship with a significant other, building student relationships takes hard work and focus. It can be all too easy to get trapped by our perspective and lose sight of this critical fact. But it will be worth it! By focusing on student relationships, you are developing a strong base for your engagement and classroom community self-efficacy and depositing a lot of capital in your thriving teacher account!

STUDENT RELATIONSHIP: REFLECTION QUESTIONS AND CHALLENGES

Consider the story of Angie Scioli and your relationships with your students as you consider the following reflection questions and the Thrive Challenge:

- How do you build authentic relationships with students?
- What characteristics do students exhibit that make it easy for you to forge relationships?
- What characteristics can challenge your ability to develop meaningful relationships?

- How have you leveraged strong relationships to challenge students and push them out of their comfort zones?
- Which dimension of care (personal, pedagogical, interpersonal) comes most naturally for you when you build relationships with students? With which dimension is there room for improvement?

STUDENT RELATIONSHIP THRIVE CHALLENGE

Make a list of all of your students. Do not use any lists, pictures, or reminders. List one thing you know about each student as a learner, a person, and a member of the classroom community. Reflect on which students you could not easily remember or for whom it was challenging to complete the list. Spend the next two weeks building relationships and repeat the process. See the example below.[5]

Student Name	As a Learner	As a Person	As a Member of the Classroom Community
Ahman	Loves to read non-fiction	Struggles with anxiety	Enjoys working in small groups
Brooke	Requires additional support with complex problem-solving	Compassionate and caring	Helps others during math

INCLUSION ACTIVATORS

Many of you are parents. If you are not a parent, you likely have kids who mean the world to you in your personal lives. As you read the following story about Liston and his excellent teachers, try to engage in the story from both your professional and personal perspectives.

- How would you define inclusion?
- Think of a thriving teacher you had when you were a student. How did you know they were a thriving teacher?
- Think of your children or children who are important to you. What do they need in a teacher?
- How does the concept of equity relate to inclusion?
- Reflect on a time when you knew of a student who exhibited behaviors that the adults in the school misunderstood. How did that make you feel? How did it make the student feel?

INCLUSION VIGNETTE:
THE POWER OF AN INCLUSIVE MINDSET

In this vignette, we will focus on Liston. Liston is a student in his neighborhood high school who enjoyed school and maintained a full class load. Liston happens to have a developmental disability impacting his cognitive processing. In addition to a rigorous course load, including classes on literature and chemistry, he is part of an anime club and co-manages the varsity basketball team.

How do Liston's teachers ensure he can find success while enjoying an enriching high school experience like all of his classmates? The answer is collaboration, adaptation, and dedication. His teachers collaborate with Liston's parents and administrators to create an inclusive program for Liston that capitalizes on his talents and abilities. This collaboration results in professional learning opportunities and plans for meaningful adaptations to Liston's instruction. Liston's team of teachers use the following guidelines to maximize inclusion:

- They lean on peers to increase meaningful social inclusion.
- They utilize Universal Design for Learning (UDL) strategies to proactively plan for success.
- They deliberately include students in the planning and transparently discuss inclusive goals.
- They include all students in the building and maintaining the classroom community by giving them meaningful roles and responsibilities.
- They lean on existing experts in their school community, thus expanding the collaborative web of support.

Liston's teachers employ many of these strategies to maximize his success. For example, his teachers shorten assignments while maintaining alignment with the standards. Liston's classmates often read to him when the goals involve understanding literature, not decoding. Often assessments are altered and offered orally. His teachers will also provide alternate learning experiences and activities to engage him along with his peers. Liston has thrived both academically and socially as a result of his thoughtful teachers and his inclusive experiences.

INCLUSION THEORY:
MODEL FOR STUDENT PARTICIPATION

The concept of inclusion is exceedingly susceptible to misinterpretation and misapplication. For this reason, a concise and relatable theoretical model is critical. Laura Lundy, co-director of the Centre for Children's Rights and a professor at Queen's University, Belfast, developed the "Lundy Model of Student Participation," a brilliant tool to conceptualize authentic and meaningful student inclusion.[6] This model informs our understanding of effective inclusive practices for all students. The Lundy model consists of four components: space, voice, audience, and influence.

- *Space:* Children must be provided safe and inclusive opportunities to develop and share their views.
- *Voice:* Children must be supported in their efforts to express their views authentically.
- *Audience:* Their voice must be authentically heard by stakeholders who have a vested interest in their students' concerns.
- *Influence:* The view of the student must influence change when appropriate.

These four elements work together interdependently to describe the conditions necessary for a meaningful and inclusive learning environment. The *space* and *voice* elements of Lundy's model describe students' right to express their views. The *audience* and *influence* elements work together to convey the students' views to be honored and considered. Although there is overlap among these four elements, *space* serves as the critical foundation. Without students being afforded a safe space to express their views, the other elements would be inaccessible.

Lundy also provides practical questions that can be asked to ensure each element of the student participation model is adequately addressed. For instance, when

The Lundy Model of Student Participation

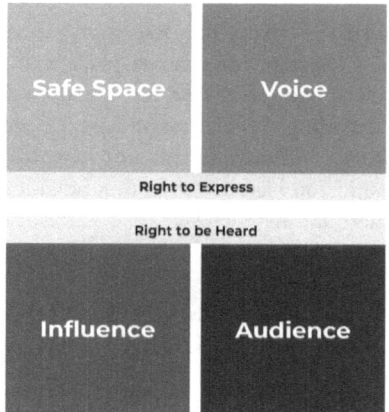

The Lundy Model of Student Participation. Laura Lundy. 2013. Adpated from *Lundy Model of Student Participation*. "'Voice' Is Not Enough: Conceptualising Article 12 of the United Nations Convention on the Rights of the Child." *British Educational Research Journal* 33(6): 927–42.[7]

considering the *space* element, you might ask, "Have children's views been actively sought?" Likewise, when considering the influence element, you might ask, "Are there procedures in place that ensure that children's views have been taken seriously?" For more specifics on Lundy's model and the checklist questions, refer to Lundy's 2007 article, "'Voice' Is Not Enough."

INCLUSION: APPLICATION TO PRACTICE

As we have read, inclusion can lead to transformative experiences for our students. This transformation is often steeped in emotion. The Lundy Model of Student Participation helped us sort through some emotions and explore the theoretical underpinning of high-quality inclusive experiences. We will now apply that understanding to allow you to leverage the power of inclusion in developing your self-efficacy. We will start with a basic definition of this concept.

Inclusive Education Canada, a national nongovernmental organization, offers a remarkably succinct and powerful definition of inclusion. "Inclusive education means that all students attend and are welcomed by their neighborhood schools in age-appropriate, regular classes and are supported to learn, contribute and participate in all aspects of the life of the school."[8] UNICEF provides an even more succinct definition: "Inclusive education means all children in the same classrooms, in the same schools."[9] Inclusive education demands that students, to the greatest extent possible, are educated in typical learning environments where all students, regardless of background or ability, have access to equitable learning experiences. These environments are not limited to classrooms and include outdoor spaces, gyms, theater spaces, cafeterias, and the community.

Notice that both of these definitions extend beyond strategies and address beliefs. We do not achieve inclusive education by simply opening our doors and dismantling isolating learning environments. We achieve inclusive education by being deliberate, intentional, results-oriented, and resolute. If we take a moment to reflect on our original definition of teacher self-efficacy, we will certainly see the direct connection to inclusion. High teacher self-efficacy is characterized by the belief that they can meet the needs of all students regardless of the challenges. The purest form of this efficacy can only be demonstrated in an inclusive environment designed to meet the needs of all students.

We do not design inclusive educational environments for any particular group of students; we create them for all. Often, conversations about inclusion are focused on students with disabilities. It is undoubtedly crucial that we design our inclusive environments with the concerns of students with disabilities in mind, but research shows that *all* students learn better in inclusive classrooms. Diversity must be valued and leveraged for all students. There are two primary manners in which you can exercise self-efficacy, enhancing inclusive practices. They include participating in inclusive classroom practices and advocating for systemic inclusion.

PARTICIPATION IN INCLUSIVE CLASSROOM PRACTICES

What can you do as a teacher to increase inclusion? If we analyze this question, it will become evident that the answer is hinged almost entirely on collaboration. We cannot simply snap our fingers and meet the needs of all of our students who may have been receiving services in segregated settings. Instead, we must find ways to harness our collective resources and redesign our system to meet the needs of our students in their neighborhood schools and their general education classrooms.

Co-teaching is a research-based strategy for increasing inclusion and is an excellent example of growing inclusion through collaboration. Co-teaching, in its purest form, consists of at least one general educator and one special educator working together to meet the needs of their shared students in the same general education environment. The most effective co-teaching also includes co-planning and co-assessment. Upon observation, the highest praise you can offer a co-teaching team is that you could not distinguish between the special educator and the general educator, and you had no idea which students had IEPs (individualized education programs).

Wendy Murawski and Wendy Lochner (2018) wrote an excellent book titled *Beyond Co-Teaching Basics: A Data-Driven, No-Fail Model for Continuous Improvement*.[10] It reads like a manual for excellence for any co-teaching implementation. In this book, Murawski and Lochner establish four Competency Domains for co-teaching, including "The Learner and Learning, The Task at Hand, Instructional Practices, and Professional Responsibilities." These domains provide a solid framework from which we can analyze our co-teaching practices.

The Learner and Learning domain addresses each student and their individual learner profile, which includes their achievement level, interests, learning styles, and preferred modes of demonstrating their learning. The Task at Hand domain addresses the curriculum concerns and goals and the compliance concerns of IEPs. The Instructional Practices domain considers the specific manner in which co-planning, co-teaching, and co-assessing will take place. Finally, the Professional Responsibilities domain addresses collaboration and communication responsibilities that are critical for co-teaching success.

How can focusing on co-teaching through the lens of the domains enhance your self-efficacy? First, let us take a broad view of the concept of co-teaching and its relationship to teacher self-efficacy. Highly efficacious teachers believe they have the necessary skills to meet the needs of all of their students. This cannot be accomplished in isolated silos. By collaborating with our colleagues, we can remove barriers and build bridges for our students. Co-teaching serves as a proven strategy to harness the power of self-efficacy, boosting collaboration effectively.

Now we can take a look at each competency domain. By focusing on the Learner and Learning domain, you bolster your engagement self-efficacy by examining the specific needs of your students and reflecting on how you can address those needs. As you address the Task at Hand and Instructional Practices domains, you build your instructional self-efficacy by adding tools to your toolbox. These tools represent the specific skills that are required for you to feel efficacious.[11]

As you explore the Professional Responsibility domain, you stand to enhance your classroom community self-efficacy and your self-care efficacy. You strengthen your classroom community as you build connections among students and consider differences as opportunities instead of deficits. You can support your self-care efficacy when you identify colleagues who support you professionally *and* personally. Co-teaching is a very structured means to engage in inclusive practices. You may or may not have the systemic support to engage in co-teaching fully. However, you can certainly increase your level of inclusion by building collaborative relationships among special and general educators.[12]

Another avenue to engage in inclusive practices is incorporating Universal Design for Learning (UDL) in your instructional design. CAST defines UDL as "a framework to improve and optimize teaching and learning for all people based on scientific insights into how humans learn."[13] UDL is based on the principle of designing your instruction to meet the needs of as many students as possible initially. Instead of simply considering instructional support for students with special needs or disabilities, UDL challenges us to think of supports that could contain obvious or hidden supports for all students.

An example of universal design outside of the world of education is closed captioning. Including closed captioning text for television shows was initially designed for people who are deaf or hard of hearing. Now, people use closed captioning to increase focus, understand accents, drown out distractions, and avoid angering their significant others by blaring the TV late at night! Here are some examples of UDL in practice in the school setting:

1. *Choice in representation:* Allowing students to represent their learning based on their preferences can be an excellent strategy to leverage their learning style. It also ensures students with learning differences are not spotlighted if their assignment does not look like everyone else's.
2. *Flexible workspace options:* Getting students out of their rows and traditional seating arrangements can allow students to collaborate when necessary, get some quiet space, or be comfortable. How many of us would sit in a plastic chair for three hours at a time if we were trying to maximize our learning?
3. *Voice to text:* Voice to text was once a high-tech trick only available to a very select few. Worse yet, lack of voice to text boxed many students out of the opportunity to produce written communication. Now voice to text can serve as a UDL support for all students to help turn their ideas into written work.
4. *Text to voice:* Now, let's flip it. Having complex text read aloud can be a great tool to allow students to comprehend complex text. Just consider the explosion of audiobook services to see just how universal this concept is becoming!

Co-teaching and UDL are two examples of ways you can increase inclusion in your learning environment. By doing so, you expand your self-efficacy by increasing the number of students you feel can find success in your classroom. This self-efficacy enhancing power of inclusion is strengthened when it is supported at the system level. We will now look at how your advocacy for system broad, inclusive practices can build your self-efficacy.

ADVOCACY FOR SYSTEMIC INCLUSION

We have examined some ways you can build self-efficacy by engaging in inclusion in your classroom. How can you advocate for more inclusion in your school, district, or beyond to expand this potential? Some teachers find that advocating for what they know is right is a great way to support their self-efficacy. You can follow this three-step process to advocate for inclusion—Step 1: Identify a Gap; Step 2: Build a Coalition; Step 3: Partner with a Change Agent.

Following this three-step process can be a self-efficacy game changer. If you can build your self-efficacy related to systemic change, you have indefinitely expanded your influence. This influence can then increase the self-efficacy of others, and the glorious process can start all over again for someone else! The first step of identifying a gap is critical as it sets the tone and direction for the entire process.

In this step of the process, you are looking for a barrier to inclusion in your school, district, or even your state. For example, you may find that all of your additional supports for struggling readers in your middle school involve having students pulled out of their classroom and receiving segregated services. You typically have to dig a little deeper to expose the gap entirely. "Why" questions serve this purpose well. Why are the services segregated? Why don't students receive support in the classroom? Why do we have so many students who require this level of support? Once these questions have been answered, you should obtain a solid view of the identified gap.

In step two, you focus on building a coalition of like-minded professionals who can help move your initiative forward. We will use the same middle school reading example to flesh this out. Again, asking yourself a few questions will help you identify possible partners. Who would have a vested interest in improving the intervention systems? How can you leverage the skills and talents of your potential coalition partners? What is your vision for the improved state of your inclusive endeavor? Once you have established the answers to these questions, you are ready to advocate for inclusion! The result of step two might be an interdisciplinary group of teachers and specialists advocating for a new schedule for the middle school that allows for common planning and co-taught services.

Step three is all about implementation. With your newly formed coalition, establish some goals. If this is a massive initiative like restructuring a department or advocating at the state level for legislative reform, creating a mission statement would prove helpful. Once you have your goals established, create a timeline with check-in meetings. Most importantly, to ensure the self-efficacy related benefits of this sort of advocacy, celebrate your efforts and your small wins as you will not necessarily accomplish your primary goal on your first attempt.

Advocacy is about influence, not control. Advocacy is about shifting perspectives, not mandating change. Teachers who reinforce their self-efficacy through advocating for inclusion realize their impact requires a long-term vision fueled by optimism and patience. Unfortunately for some, advocacy can negatively impact self-efficacy by not generating the quick wins some need. If you are looking for an advocacy platform, ensure that you are ready to exert your influence with passion and vision patiently.

INCLUSION: REFLECTION QUESTIONS

1. One of the Activators for this chapter asked you to define inclusion. After reading this section, would you change anything in your definition of inclusion?
2. Which of the four elements in Lundy's model (Space, Voice, Audience, or Influence) do you most naturally facilitate with your students? Why do you think this is the case?
3. Which of the four elements do you find most challenging?
4. What is the greatest success you have had related to inclusive practices?
   a. How did that success impact your self-efficacy?
   b. How can you replicate that success?
5. If you were to advocate for a change in your school, district, or state related to inclusion, what would it be? Are you ready to build a coalition?

INCLUSION THRIVE CHALLENGE

Identify one upcoming lesson that you think some students might find challenging or inaccessible. Consider the framework for UDL to redesign the lesson by:

- Altering the way students engage;
- Reconsidering the way you represent the information; and
- Offering voice and choice in the way students can represent their learning.

When you have completed the lesson, reflect on how your lesson design impacted student learning.

5

The Self-Care Paradox

We have spent a great deal of time exploring the five factors that contribute to the development of your self-efficacy. While it is undoubtedly true that a thriving teacher must possess high levels of self-efficacy in student engagement, instruction, and classroom community, we must recognize all of the factors are intensely emotionally demanding. Therefore, it is time to address the elephant in the room, namely the self-care paradox. By dedicating your professional life to the continuous improvement and ever-increasing efficacy discussed thus far, you run the risk of emptying your tank and flirting with the career killer of teacher burnout.

The research of the link between teacher self-efficacy and burnout is fascinating. Most existing research suggests that high levels of teacher self-efficacy mitigate the risk of burnout.

There is also, however, growing research suggesting high levels of self-efficacy, if unchecked, can lead to burnout. This relationship between high self-efficacy and burnout is driven by teaching. Believing in your heart that you have what it takes to meet the varied needs of all your students is a daunting task that can be unsustainable. Therefore, it is imperative that you take care of yourself.

The concept of self-care is not new, but it is gaining more bandwidth in the professional literature and discourse. The Global Self-Care Federation defines self-care as "the practice of individuals looking after their health using the knowledge and information available to them. It is a decision-making process that empowers individuals to look after their health efficiently and conveniently, in collaboration with health and social care professionals as needed."[1] Self-care is multidimensional and looks different for everybody. Some common elements include:

- Nutrition
- Stress management
- Social supports including family and friends
- Physical activity and fitness
- Sleep
- Contribution to others
- Connection to a higher power

SELF-CARE ACTIVATORS

1. What do you do to maintain a work-life balance?
2. What situations or circumstances throw your work-life balance off-kilter?
3. What is something you wish you could do in your personal life that you do not have time to do due to your professional responsibilities?
4. Think of one teacher you admire who seems to have high teacher self-efficacy AND maintains a healthy work-life balance. What is one thing you could emulate from this teacher?
5. When during the school year do you feel most at peace? Why?

SELF-CARE: APPLICATION TO PRACTICE

Emotional self-care can be challenging for teachers and others in caregiving professions. When we have been programmed (by others and ourselves) that our job is to care for others at any cost, that cost is often our own emotional well-being. Teachers' willingness to engage in efficient and consistent self-care practices can also be hindered by a common misconception of what self-care is really all about.

Outdated and inaccurate representations of the true meaning of self-care include indulgent spa treatments, sugary coffee drinks, and expensive excursions. This is not meant to suggest those practices are not worthwhile, but they are not realistic self-care. Self-care is about mindfulness and discipline. We must commit to consistently taking the time to care for ourselves.

Prioritizing: The first and most critical step in developing a self-care regimen is establishing your priorities. You must find ways to prioritize yourself. That is not being selfish. Instead, it will make you a better teacher. By establishing priorities, you will balance the need to take care of yourself while providing exceptional service to your students. Considering the adage "do the first things first" might prove helpful when you engage in your prioritization process.

Dwight Eisenhower developed a conceptual framework while serving as a general in the United States Army and as the Supreme Commander of Allied Expeditionary Forces during World War II. This concept is now known as the Eisenhower Principle.[2] He developed the principle to help himself and his teams differentiate between urgent and important matters. We can use this matrix to help us prioritize. Essentially, the principle established that all matters we must address have a degree of importance and a degree of urgency. Eisenhower frequently spoke to the critical nature of prioritizing important over urgent. Stephen Covey developed the matrix based on the principles expressed by Eisenhower. This handy tool can help us avoid the trap of chasing the urgent matters all day long and completely losing sight of the important.[3]

The Eisenhower Matrix

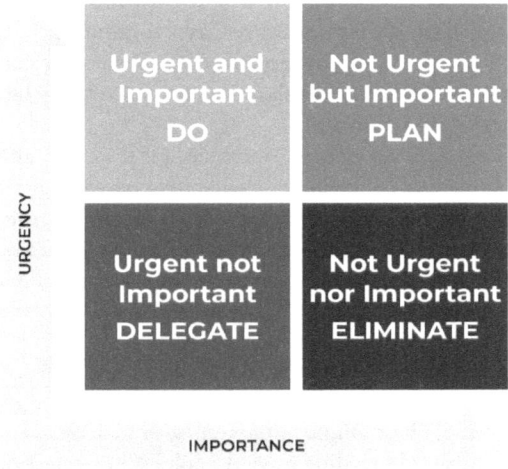

The Eisenhower Matrix. Stephen A. Covey, Roger Merrill, and Rebecca Merrill. The Eisenhower Matrix. Based on information from First Things First: To Live, to Love, to Learn, to Leave a Legacy. (New York: Simon and Schuster, 1994), p 32.[4]

Urgency is a measure of the demand for immediate attention. Importance is a measure of how directly a matter is linked to our strategic goals. These are not value judgments as we must attend to the urgent and the important. It goes without saying that tasks that are both urgent and important demand the most immediate and thoughtful consideration. This is why they earn the "Do!" designation. Attend to these tasks post haste. The "Not Urgent but Important" quadrant is critical but can inadvertently be put on the back burner. Not only do these tasks require *planning* but you must also *plan* to do these tasks! One helpful tactic is to actually put these tasks on your calendar; otherwise, the less important tasks will undoubtedly creep into all available white space on your daily agenda.[5]

The following two quadrants represent tasks with low levels of importance. If the task at hand is urgent but not important, for example, phone calls and emails, do your best to delegate or systematize. If you have the luxury of delegating, that is great. However, this may not be possible—if not, systematize. For example, you might create a system where you agree to check all emails from 4:30 to 5:00 before you go home. This might have you at work a little longer, but it could amplify your presence in the classroom and at home. We will keep the last one simple. If the task is neither urgent nor important, stop doing it![6]

As discussed earlier, self-care requires discipline. It would be relatively easy to focus on your priorities for a few weeks (consider New Year's resolutions), but sustained focus on self-care requires serious self-discipline. A high level of self-discipline can help us balance the priority of self-care with the need to care deeply for our students. Unfortunately, self-care is often portrayed as self-indulgence. Resist this damaging stigma, as it will surely erode your discipline by erroneously making you feel selfish. If you prioritize self-care and find balance, there will actually be more of you to offer to others, especially your students.

Self-Care Strategies: Once you have established priorities and developed the discipline to maintain your focus on your self-care, you can adopt strategies that work for you. Self-care is incredibly personal. What works for one teacher may make another teacher experience increased stress. For example, many teachers find meditating impossibly stressful while others find their Zen through a strict meditation regimen. There are two primary self-care strategies we will examine—"unplugging" and "plugging in."

Unplugging strategies are those that allow you to disconnect from external stimuli and focus quietly on your own thoughts and emotions. These strategies tend to work better for introverts. These unplugging strategies include meditation, mindfulness practices, and even simply reading a good book. When selecting potential opportunities to unplug, it is important to be deliberate. Unplugging should not be used as a way to avoid unpleasant but important work. I highly recommend scheduling your opportunity to unplug. Fifteen minutes a day can go a long way!

Plugging in refers to the self-care activities that get you involved in a social activity that recharges your battery and allows you to do something you *want* to do, rather than something you *need* to do. These are often the go-to self-care strategies for extroverts. It is best to identify self-care strategies that enhance your overall well-being. You do not want to rely on "self-care" strategies that may be enjoyable but have a negative impact on other aspects of your life. There is certainly nothing wrong with enjoying an adult beverage with friends from time to time, but this should not be your only approach to self-care.

Whatever style of self-care you select, make sure it feeds your soul. We previously explored the importance of establishing priorities as part of your journey to sustainable self-care. If your self-care strategies align with your priorities, you have struck gold. For many of us, our families are a top priority. Sometimes, we find ourselves only able to spend time with our children as spectators or chauffeurs. For folks in this category, carving out a once-a-week game night might be an excellent addition to the self-care regimen as it feeds your soul and priorities.

We will close out this section by revisiting the story of Angie Scioli, the subject of the documentary *Teacher of the Year*. Before the decision was made to include Angie's inspirational and authentic story demonstrating her gift for establishing enriching relationships with students, I reached out to her to make sure she was comfortable with me referencing her story. Angie graciously allowed me to include her story in this book.

Ms. Scioli also told me that she was planning on retiring earlier than she had intended. She felt the weight of getting up at 3:00 AM to grade papers and spending Saturday mornings writing college letters of recommendation for her students. It is cause for celebration when teachers retire on top of their game, feeling satisfied with their life's work. Angie's description of her decision to retire might leave you feeling melancholy.[7]

Angie should be nothing but proud of her service to her students. She is a fantastic teacher worthy of the distinction of Teacher of the Year. Great teachers should not feel they cannot realistically balance the demands of parenthood and teaching. It is not fair to teachers, our students, or our kids. I am encouraged by the increased focus on teacher self-care in recent years. If we genuinely want our nation's schools filled with self-efficacious teachers who maintain their vigor throughout their careers, we must remain steadfast in our commitment to teachers' well-being.

This chapter opened by examining the first self-care paradox. Namely, all factors that build teacher self-efficacy require massive levels of dedication, energy, and perseverance. These factors can, for some, deplete the energy we have in store for our families and ourselves. There is another self-care paradox. Quite simply, self-care cannot be adequately maintained by yourself. We need systems of support for our teachers to give them access and permission to focus on themselves for the benefit of our students.

SELF-CARE REFLECTION

1. On a scale of 1–5 (1 being low), how would you rate your discipline related to your self-care?
2. Do you gravitate toward "unplugging" or "plugging-in" self-care strategies?
3. What is one activity or ritual you use for self-care?
4. When was the last time you engaged in this activity? If it has been too long, why?
5. What is one thing you have always wanted to do but for which you struggled to find the time?

SELF-CARE CHALLENGE

It is time to commit to self-care by creating a self-care plan. There are plenty of resources out there to guide you through this process more precisely. Below you can find an abbreviated self-care development plan. It is a simple approach to get you started.

- *Step 1:* Identify your stressors.
- *Step 2:* Use the Eisenhower Principle to determine if these stressors are indeed important.

- *Step 3:* Determine which domains of self-care require attention (emotional, physical, spiritual, mental, or social).
- *Step 4:* Identify strategies that have worked for you in the past to improve your self-care.
- *Step 5:* Schedule at least 15 minutes per day for these strategies. I also encourage at least a one-hour block at some point for you to pursue a passion.
- *Step 6:* Find an accountability partner to ensure your discipline to your adherence to this plan.

6

The Career Stages of a Thriving Teacher

It is time to start planning *your* journey. This section allows you to develop a personal itinerary for your trip toward a thriving teaching career. No two teachers' journeys are entirely alike, so it is critical to find what works for you. When you have completed this section, you will have a solid understanding of where you are in your journey, and you will have identified the next steps that will help you build and maintain your teacher self-efficacy.

The two models described in this chapter will ground you in the critical concepts that support teacher self-efficacy through a long and rewarding career. The first model you will explore is the Thriving Teacher Model. This model describes the four domains of teacher self-efficacy and the general levels of efficacy within each domain.

Second, you will learn about the Focus and Influence Model, which describes the two general forces that propel teachers toward increased and supported self-efficacy. Then you will complete two inventories that will generate scores that represent your predispositions related to two essential factors. The first set of scores describes your tendencies related to the Five Thrive Factors. These are the research-based factors that have been demonstrated to support teacher self-efficacy. The second set of data describes your general tendencies in the four domains of teacher self-efficacy, including student engagement, instruction, classroom community, and self-care.

Imagine sitting at a staff meeting led by a principal who wants to improve student learning outcomes. The principal announces to all the teachers that he will focus on instructional practices, student engagement, and classroom community by doing rounds and providing feedback and direction for everyone.

Picture this principal walking into your classroom and asking you to sort your students into groups based on your level of instructional self-efficacy. The principal asks you to create groups based on your belief in meeting their instructional needs. The principal says, "If you are pretty sure you cannot reach them instructionally, have them sit over in the corner so you can focus on those you think you can reach." You reluctantly abide by this bizarre suggestion and later let your principal know that this did not help you or your students for obvious reasons.

The next day the principal walks in and says," We are going to switch up this grouping. It seems we have some behavior issues. Now sort them by your belief in your ability to manage their behavior. This should make it easier for you to focus where you feel successful." You listen to your principal in disbelief and later follow up with a very similar description of your day that you previously offered. It did not work.

On the third day, your principal walks in and says, "I have a new idea. It is clearly about engagement. Sort these kids based on your belief in your ability to meaningfully engage them in the learning process. If you can't engage them, stick them over there in the corner." You are perplexed.

On the fourth day, your administrator calls an emergency staff meeting. He says, "I have been stopping in all of your classrooms and giving you advice on how you can create a more efficient learning environment. In the past three days, I have tried to address instruction, classroom community, and engagement, but it does not seem to be working. Unfortunately, I've seen anxiety on the rise, teachers coming into my office tell me they feel like they're burning out, and more sick days used than I have seen in a long time. Clearly, I have to do something about this. To make this easier for me, please sort yourselves in groups based on your ability to manage your emotions and maintain a growth mindset."

This nightmare scenario would certainly never genuinely manifest. Teachers and school administrators would never act in such a way, but there are two important lessons embedded in this little drama. First, it is not uncommon for schools, in order to try to meet the needs of our students, to segregate and silo them into programs that ultimately erode teacher self-efficacy. Second, these four scenarios represent the four domains of teacher self-efficacy: instructional efficacy, student engagement efficacy, classroom community efficacy, and self-care efficacy. Although there are strategies to address each domain of teacher self-efficacy, it is critical we take a holistic view and realize these domains are interconnected. Teacher self-efficacy is about believing one can meet the needs of all students. We cannot support teacher self-efficacy by accepting that it is good enough to focus on a certain subset of students as described in the previous drama. We need to support the development of self-efficacy for all teachers at all career stages so we can unleash the potential of our greatest educational asset: great teachers.

Megan Tschannen-Moran and Anita Woolfolk Hoy established a powerful model for teacher self-efficacy that hundreds of scholars from myriad perspectives have studied.[1] Their teacher self-efficacy model established three aspects of teacher self-efficacy: instruction, classroom management, and student engagement. The modified model you will explore in this chapter contains some adaptations and additions.

Most notably, this model includes a fourth domain of teacher self-efficacy related to self-care. This addition addresses the concern raised by some research suggesting elevated teacher self-efficacy can actually contribute to burnout. In addition, classroom management has been adjusted to represent a more inclusive perspective as classroom community. This model holds that thriving teachers believe in their ability to build community with their students, engage them, and provide impactful instruction while taking care of themselves and maintaining work-life balance.

The Thriving Teacher Model consists of three levels of self-efficacy for each of the four domains. Each level is characterized by the circumstances in which teachers at that level would feel efficacious. The levels include emerging, expanding, and thriving.

The emerging level describes the earliest development of self-efficacy in which teachers only truly feel efficacious in relatively undemanding circumstances. The expanding level describes a state in which the teacher believes in their ability to be successful within increasingly complex and demanding circumstances. Finally, at the thriving level, teachers feel efficacious in the most complex situations and maintain a growth mindset regardless of the challenges they face. These states are dynamic as self-efficacy can ebb and flow for all teachers, no matter how skilled, experienced, or positive they might be.

INSTRUCTION

It is hard to argue that delivering high-quality instruction for all students is not a fundamental aspect of a teaching career. Possessing a high level of instructional self-efficacy does not mean every lesson you provide is perfect and all students meet the intended objectives. It means that you believe you have the skills to deliver meaningful instruction for all students. Strong instructional self-efficacy supports resilience by accepting that less-than-stellar lessons are part of the teaching and learning process while maintaining a belief that the next lesson will be more potent. Below you will find the three levels of instructional self-efficacy. Each level is described by the circumstances and conditions in which teachers at the given level will feel efficacious.

- *Emerging Instructional Efficacy: Proficient.* At the emerging level of instructional self-efficacy, teachers believe they have the ability and skills to provide appropriate and practical instruction for students who have already become proficient. However, when faced with students who require more support to reach proficiency, their self-belief wanes. Remember that this does not mean that they do not have the requisite skills. Self-efficacy is a measure of a belief, not an actual skill.
- *Expanding Instructional Efficacy: Approaching Grade-Level.* At the expanding level of instructional efficacy, teachers' belief in their instructional skills broadens. Teachers at this level believe they can not only meet the instructional needs of students who are already proficient but also those who need additional support. Thus, these teachers are not entirely dependent on prepackaged programs

or scripted curriculum. Instead, they can adapt more nimbly to meet the needs of students who need a little more.
- *Thriving Instructional Efficacy: All Academic Levels of Performance.* Teachers at the thriving level of instructional efficacy believe they have the necessary skills to meet the needs of students in their class regardless of their learning needs. But, more importantly, teachers at this level embrace the diverse needs of their students and feed their self-efficacy by designing and delivering the instruction to meet their needs.

CLASSROOM COMMUNITY

- *Emerging Classroom Community Efficacy: Homogeneous.* Teachers at the emerging level of classroom community efficacy have doubts about their ability to build classroom community except under the most idyllic circumstances. When students do not enter the learning environment with the skills and predispositions to work together effectively, teachers at this level question their ability to foster a high-functioning learning community. Teachers at this level can succumb to the risk of blaming students for a struggling learning community.
- *Expanding Classroom Community Efficacy: Limited Challenges.* Teachers at the expanding level of classroom community efficacy accept their responsibility to develop a collaborative and robust classroom community. When run-of-the-mill challenges arise related to a smoothly functioning classroom community, teachers at this level believe they have the skills to make the necessary adjustments to right the ship.
- *Thriving Classroom Community Efficacy: Any Classroom Mix.* Teachers at the thriving level of classroom community efficacy find motivation and inspiration by the challenge of creating a robust and student-centered classroom community. They refuse to blame a student for behaviors or actions that challenge the classroom community. Instead, they focus on proactive strategies to support all students and rely on restorative practices when they need to respond.

STUDENT ENGAGEMENT

- *Emerging Student Engagement Efficacy: Compliant.* Teachers at the emerging level of student engagement only honestly believe they have the skills to engage compliant students. These teachers often view student engagement as an inherent ability of the student. They indirectly blame families, students, or society for the lack of engagement they experience in their classroom.
- *Expanding Student Engagement Efficacy: Interested.* Teachers at the expanding level of student engagement efficacy believe it is their responsibility to engage students in the learning process and they feel efficacious as long as the students

are interested in what the teacher is presenting or facilitating. These classrooms tend to be teacher-centered. Teachers at this level sometimes mistake entertainment for engagement. They focus on creating learning experiences that students enjoy but lack full regard for deep and meaningful engagement.
- *Thriving Student Engagement Efficacy: All Students.* Teachers at the thriving level of student engagement efficacy create student-centered learning environments. They believe in their ability to engage all students in the learning experiences. They create personalized learning environments where student agency is held at a premium. Students with teachers at this level are driving their learning.

SELF-CARE

- *Emerging Self-Care Efficacy: Normal Circumstances.* Teachers at the emerging level of self-care efficacy believe they have the skills to balance the pressures and stress of a teaching profession under normal circumstances with limited challenges.
- *Expanding Self-Care Efficacy: Daily Challenges.* Teachers at the expanding level of self-care efficacy believe they can take care of themselves when they experience typical daily challenges. These teachers employ proactive and responsive strategies to navigate the challenges of a teaching profession and maintain their work-life balance.
- *Thriving Self-Care Efficacy: Crisis.* Teachers at the thriving level of self-care efficacy look very much like teachers at the expanding level until crisis hits. When

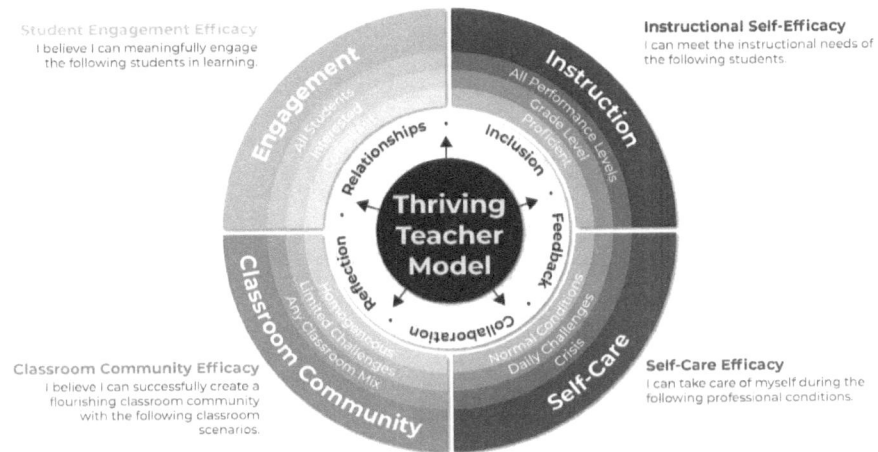

Thriving Teacher Model. David Grambow. *Thriving Teacher Model.* 2021.[2]

the school community experiences crisis, teachers at the thriving level of self-care efficacy emerge as leaders. Other teachers and staff members in the school community turn to these teachers to guide the healing process. As they provide stabilizing leadership to their learning community, their self-efficacy blossoms.

THE FOCUS AND INFLUENCE MODEL

Teachers improve their self-efficacy by harnessing the power of refined focus and expanded influence. As thriving teachers progress through their careers, they gradually shift their focus from themselves to individual students. This is not to suggest that new teachers are not student-focused. Instead, research indicates that the actions of novice teachers do not necessarily match their student-focused aspirations. Nor does this mean that all teachers progress to the highest level of the refined focus continuum. Some teachers progress more quickly than others, while others never reach the pinnacle or they leave the profession before they have the opportunity to do so.

Some thriving teachers progress through their careers and directly enhance their self-efficacy by finding opportunities to exercise more significant influence. However, all teachers must begin their careers by building their skills and finding their

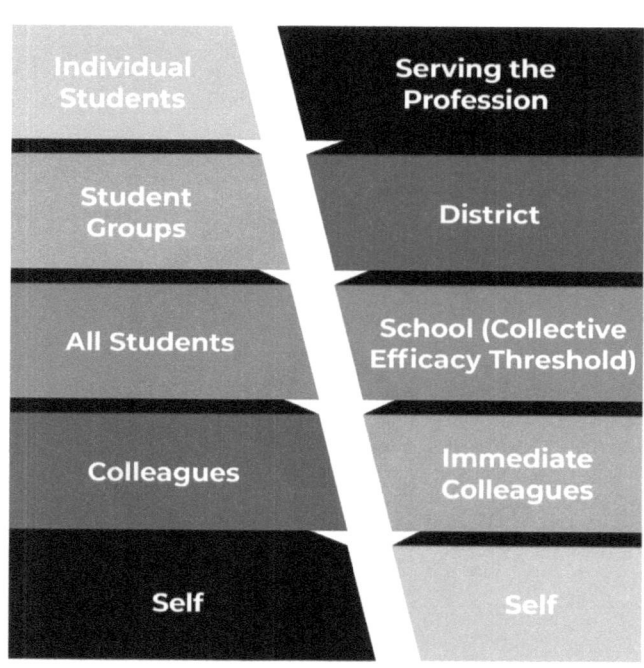

The Focus and Influence Model. David Grambow. *The Focus and Influence Model*. 2021.

place in their school culture. They do this by taking risks and stepping outside their comfort zones, taking incremental steps outside their existing spheres of influence, and providing leadership for an ever-expanding audience.

The focus and influence continua serve as the fuel that energizes teachers to develop and refine their skills in each of the Five Thrive Factors. For instance, as thriving teachers progress through their careers, their reflective skills shift from focusing on their teaching to a more refined focus on individual students. Likewise, a thriving teacher's sphere of influence related to the inclusive practices factor may expand from a small group of trusted colleagues to a large social media following. The fuel of focus and influence, as described in this model, are very personalized. No two teachers rely on focus or influence precisely the same. This model should serve you as you develop a deeper understanding of what feeds your self-efficacy.

THE REFINED FOCUS CONTINUUM

As you examine the refined focus side of the continuum, reflect on your level of focus. Later, you will have the opportunity to complete an inventory that will assist you in identifying your predispositions related to your level of focus and influence in each of the related Thrive Factors. To activate your schema, consider the following questions as you read through this section:

- How do you balance the need to think about your teaching and your students' learning?
- How has this evolved as you have progressed through your career?
- What limits your ability to focus on individual students as much as you would like?
- How might you overcome these limiting factors?

1. *Focus on Self:* The first few years of teaching can be overwhelming. New teachers must focus on learning the curriculum, understanding the culture, and becoming acclimated to the programs available to students. As a result, they find themselves filling their day (and much of the evening) simply figuring out what they will do next. This is not a value judgment, and it is an essential step in a teacher's professional development.
2. *Focus on Colleagues:* The team with which a new teacher finds themselves working is the most critical support structure available. A strong team of teachers who understands the needs of their new colleagues can offer direct support. They can also allow for a crucial kind of indirect support by allowing their new colleague to take risks in an emotionally safe environment. New teachers often rely heavily on their new teams to the point that they emulate many of their practices. This allows the new teachers to focus on new strategies without the time and energy that the subsequent few phases require.

3. *Focus on All Students:* At a certain point in most teachers' careers, they learn to shift their focus from the adult actions toward student need. At the most basic level of a focus on students, teachers concentrate on the needs of all students. At this point in a teacher's professional growth, their self-efficacy is boosted as they shift their focus from what they do as a teacher to how their students respond.
4. *Focus on Student Groups:* Teachers know from their very first field experience opportunities that not all students need precisely the same thing. Skilled and experienced teachers know how to focus their efforts on small groups of students with similar needs to increase their efficiency and effectiveness. This can come in the form of small-group instruction, small social skills groups, or any other of a number of strategies that increase the level of specificity from the whole class to small groups.
5. *Focus on Individual Students:* At the most advanced level, the focus shifts from whole class and small group to the individual needs of each student. This is a very humanistic approach as teachers' concerns at this level often shift from pure academics to helping each student maximize their potential socially, emotionally, and academically. As is the case in the previous two levels, thriving teachers do not look to find someone else to meet the needs of their students. Instead, they either try their best to meet the needs alone or collaborate with others to meet those needs.

THE EXPANDING INFLUENCE CONTINUUM

1. *Influence on Self:* It is no coincidence that the lowest level of each continuum relates to self. Novice teachers must focus on their skill development, and they need to exercise self-influence to continue to progress. Self-influence is a broad term that applies to more familiar concepts such as self-control, self-restraint, and self-motivation. Teachers in this stage begin to develop their self-identity as professionals. Although influenced by others, the influence they exert is limited to themselves.
2. *Influence on Immediate Colleagues:* Exercising expanding influence can be intimidating for new teachers who are still cognitively testing their ideas about instruction and student support. Just as teachers begin to focus on the work of their immediate colleagues, they begin to test their influence on them. Influencing colleagues can occur in the safest emotional spaces where new teachers feel free to step outside of their comfort zones and attempt to get others to see and understand something the way they do. This sort of influence can take place with a professional learning community team, a curricular team, a grade-level team, or even with a group of similarly experienced teachers.
3. *Influence on School:* John Hattie, world-renowned educational researcher, recently updated his list of the highly correlated influences on student learning.

He identified collective efficacy as the new number one influence on student learning. Collective efficacy is the shared belief of staff in their ability to impact student learning positively. When teachers expand their influence to the school level, they are poised to impact collective efficacy and increase the likelihood of all students in the school of finding success.
4. *Influence on the District:* Not all teachers get to the point where they desire to impact beyond the school in which they work. Others never have the opportunity, given the structures in their district. For some, however, the expansion of influence at the district level feeds their self-efficacy. This can come from influencing policy, writing curriculum, or taking on an official leadership role such as an instructional coach.
5. *Influence on Profession as a Whole:* Some teachers are so impassioned to affect transformational change that their self-efficacy requires institutional influence to be fed. Research suggests that this is the least common of all ten categories of focus or influence. For some, this takes the form of political activism for educational causes. For others, participation in a professional organization fits the bill.

When we consider these two continua, it is important to understand that they are cumulative. This means you do not abandon the previous focus or influence. Instead, we simply add to our repertoire of opportunities to support our self-efficacy. For instance, a teacher who seeks to bolster their self-efficacy by refining their focus to individual students does not forgo strategies for small group instruction. We will examine this phenomenon as we explore our first factor of self-reflection from a career perspective.

THE THRIVE FACTOR INVENTORIES

To prepare for a more personalized experience as you progress through the five subsequent chapters, you will complete the Thrive Factor Inventory. You will use the results of this inventory to focus your reading and chart your path toward a thriving career.

The Thrive Factor Inventory will provide insight into the level at which you generally operate with each factor. You will be able to leverage this new understanding to map your path toward a thriving career. As you complete the inventory, remember that this is your perception, and this information is only for you. Be as honest as possible with yourself to truly reap the benefits of this tool. Once you respond to each statement on the inventory by rating the degree to which you agree, add up the points in each column.

Directions for the Thrive Factor Inventory

The purpose of the Thrive Factor Inventory is to examine the way you leverage each of the Five Thrive Factors to build and maintain your self-efficacy. You will generate four scores per factor. They will include a score for each of the three factor levels of each factor and a total for all factors. Your total by level will give you a general idea of which level you currently operate for each factor. The total by factor will provide you with a sense of the factors you lean on most heavily. You will use this information to inform your plans for progressing through your journey toward a rewarding and efficacious career.

Part I: The Thrive Factor Inventory

Use the following five-point scale to indicate the degree to which you agree with each statement.
1=Strongly Disagree
2=Disagree
3=Neutral
4=Agree
5=Strongly Agree

Factor	Item #	Statement
Self-Reflection	1	Colleagues regularly seek me out to enhance their reflection.
	2	I have the skills to reflect on my students' learning to personalize my instruction for individual students in my class.
	3	I regularly advocate for professional learning for myself and others related to self-reflection.
	4	I have the skills to reflect on my teaching to improve instruction for groups of students in my class.
	5	I have the skills to reflect on my students' learning to improve instruction during a lesson.
	6	I have the skills to reflect on my teaching to improve instruction for individual students in my class.
Feedback	7	I am skilled at adjusting my instruction based on positive feedback from my supervisor.
	8	I systematically improve my instruction based on critical feedback from my colleagues.
	9	I systematically improve my instruction based on positive feedback from my colleagues.
	10	I am skilled at adjusting my instruction based on critical feedback from my supervisor.
	11	I am skilled at adjusting my instruction based on critical feedback from my students.
	12	I am skilled at improving my instruction based on positive feedback from my students.
Inclusion	13	I am a leader in the area of inclusion and differentiation.
	14	I rely on the mentorship of others.
	15	I regularly coach other teachers who are looking for advice.
	16	I regularly seek advice from trusted mentors.
	17	I participate in professional networks and organizations focused on meeting the needs of students.
	18	I rely on my colleagues to meet the needs of my students.
Relationships	19	I find it difficult to challenge a student to the point of discomfort.
	20	I have the skills to challenge resistant students to grow.
	21	It is important that my students like and respect me.
	22	I have skills to help students resolve conflicts resulting in stronger student-to-student relationships.
	23	I have the skills to teach all kids to collaborate.
	24	I systematically build my students' belief in their own abilities.
Collaboration	25	I am motivated by supporting my students with behavioral challenges.
	26	I feel confident in my abilities to help all students reach their goals.
	27	I am motivated by supporting my students with academic challenges.
	28	I optimize the potential of my students with disabilities.
	29	I am viewed as a leader in the area of inclusive teaching.
	30	I regularly advocate for more inclusive practices in my district.

The Thrive Factory Inventory. Based on concepts developed by Megan Tschannen-Moran and Anita-Woolfolk-Hoy.[3]

Theme/Level	Level 1	Level 2	Level 3	Totals by Factor
Self-Reflection (Items 1-6)				
Feedback (Items 7-12)				
Inclusion (Items 13-18)				
Student-Relationships (Items 19-24)				
Collaboration (Items 25-30)				

Direction for Part II Thrive Domain:

The purpose of Part II is to examine your relative strengths related to each of the Thrive Domains. As a reminder, the Thrive Domains are the four areas in which thriving teachers can feel efficacious. You will generate one score per domain and a total Thrive score. The individual domain scores will provide you with some insight into which domain you feel most confident. You will generate a score from four to twenty per domain. The higher the score, the more efficacious you likely feel in each particular domain. The total Thrive score will provide you with a score from four to eighty. The higher the score, the more generally efficacious you feel like a teacher. We will use this information throughout the next five chapters.

Part II: The Thrive Domain Inventory

Use the following five-point scale to indicate the degree to which you agree with each statement.

1=Strongly Disagree
2=Disagree
3=Neutral
4=Agree
5=Strongly Agree

Item #	PART II – Thrive Domains	Skill Level	Skill Level	Skill Level	Skill Level
1	I have the skills to co-construct rules and norms with my students.				
2	I am the best-suited teacher to meet the learning needs of my students with significant social-emotional challenges.				
3	I share the responsibility to engage my students with their families and my administrators.				
4	I have the skills to navigate a long and rewarding career as a teacher.				
5	I have the ability to maintain a work-life balance.				

6	I am motivated by students who need additional support to meet expectations.				
7	My students learn more when I have more diverse learners (including ethnicity, race, learning skills, socio-economics, etc...)				
8	I am the best-suited teacher to meet the learning needs of my students with significant learning challenges.				
9	I am motivated by students who are challenging to engage.				
10	I am solely responsible for my students' level of engagement.				
11	I can remain present for my students, my families, my friends, and myself.				
12	Colleagues view me as a leader when addressing cultural perspectives of their students and families in their teaching.				
13	I can build strong relationships with my students' families and improve as a teacher because of those relationships.				
14	During a crisis, my colleagues can count on me for inspiration and positivity.				
15	Colleagues seek me out to identify strategies to engage resistant students.				
16	Other teachers seek me out to provide leadership related to best-practice instruction.				
	Classroom Community Skill Score				
	Instruction Self-Efficacy Score				
	Student Engagement Self-Efficacy Score				
	Self-Care Self-Efficacy Score				
	Total Thrive Score				

The Thrive Domain Inventory. Based on concepts developed by Megan Tschannen-Moran and Anita-Woolfolk-Hoy.[4]

Personal Thrive Summary Table Directions

The purpose of this table is to provide you with easy access to the data you will use in each of the next five chapters. To complete this table, transfer the related data from the two inventories on the previous pages.

Personal Thrive Summary Table				
Thrive Factors (Part I)	**Score**			
	Level 1	Level 2	Level 3	Total
Self-Reflection				
Feedback				
Collaboration				
Student-Relationships				
Inclusion				
Thrive Domains (Part II)	**Score**			
Classroom Community Self-Efficacy				
Instruction Self-Efficacy				
Student Engagement Self-Efficacy				
Self-Care Self-Efficacy				
Total of Thrive Domain Scores				

To complete an interactive electronic version of this inventory, visit the Teacher Efficacy Network at: https://www.teacherefficacynetwork.com/inventory.

To complete an interactive electronic version of this inventory, visit the Teacher Efficacy Network at: https://www.teacherefficacynetwork.com/courses.

The purpose of this table is to provide you with easy access to the data you will use in each of the following five chapters. To complete this table, transfer the related data from the two inventories. Mark this page to keep it handy, as you will be using it periodically as you navigate the next few chapters.

Personal Thrive Summary Table				
Thrive Factors (Part I)	Score			
	Stage 1	Stage 2	Stage 3	Total
Self-Reflection				
Feedback				
Collaboration				
Student Relationships				
Inclusion				
Thrive Domains (Part II)	Score			
Classroom Community Self-Efficacy				
Instruction Self-Efficacy				
Student Engagement Self-Efficacy				
Self-Care Self-Efficacy				
Total of Thrive Domain Scores				

Your bags are packed with the understanding of the Thrive Factors and your own predispositions. Now it is time for you to explore the next phase of your Thriving Teacher journey. Each of the following five chapters will provide you with an overview of the developmental career stages for each of the Five Thrive Factors. Your first destination on the journey is self-reflection.

7
Self-Reflection Career Stages

When we travel, we set out to create experiences. We want to see, hear, taste, and feel emotions we may not be able to if we retreat to our comfort zone. When we create these experiences, we do not intend to forget them when we return home. We create memories. Memories gain their meaning through reflection. We look at pictures, recall stories, and reminisce about especially meaningful moments in our travel. Reflection also helps thriving teachers as they navigate their self-efficacy journeys.

In your previous exploration in chapter 1, you learned that self-reflection serves as the foundational factor for teacher self-efficacy. Reflection is a cognitive tool you can use to assist in every level of your decision-making. Thinking about your practice without adjusting practice based on your insight is not a true reflection and does not generate the self-efficacy boosting benefits.

You also learned that self-reflection exists on a continuum from casual to formal and on another continuum from reflection-on-action to reflection-in-action. You reflected on your tendencies and informally evaluated your self-reflection using these two continua. Understanding where your reflective tendencies land on these continua is an important first step in unleashing the self-efficacy related benefits of reflection. Quite simply, teachers without strong reflective practices cannot fully leverage the other four Thrive Factors to maximize their self-efficacy.

This chapter will explore how teachers can progress through the three stages of self-reflection as they gain experience. The three stages of self-reflection include teacher-focused reflection, student-focused reflection, and reflective leadership. You will develop an understanding of where you are on the continuum of self-reflection development. You will also be challenged to identify opportunities to propel your development forward as you expand your self-reflective capacity.

Teachers can progress through three stages of self-reflection development. Stage 1 is teacher-focused reflection. Teachers practicing teacher-focused reflection spend the majority of their reflective energies focusing on the actions of teachers. Stage 2 is student-focused reflection. At this level, teachers turn their reflective energies toward considering the learning behaviors of their students. Stage 3 is reflective leadership.

At this level, teachers unleash the power of their reflection to help other teachers refine their craft and critically consider other perspectives.

Teacher-Focused Reflection	Student-Focused Reflection	Reflective Leadership
Adult-Centric	Student-Centric	Student-Centric
Prioritizes Improved Instruction	Prioritizes Student Learning	Prioritizes Perspectives of Others
Episodic	Cyclical	Episodic or Cyclical
Reactive	Responsive	Responsive
Cooperative	Collaborative	Empowering

Self-reflection can support all four domains of self-efficacy. For example, if your reflection is focused on instruction, it is likely to impact instructional self-efficacy. The same logic applies to the other three domains of self-efficacy. In each section, you will be presented with questions encouraging you to consider how reflection can support your development of self-efficacy in all four domains.

Before you continue your exploration, it is time to pause and reflect on your Thriving Teacher Inventory results. Remember that these results are not evaluative, nor are they scientific. Instead, they are designed to inspire self-reflection and activate schema as you explore each of the Five Thrive Factors. First, complete the table below with the corresponding results from the inventory. Once you have completed the table, you will learn how to use the results to maximize the impact of your reflection.

Personal Thrive Summary Table				
Thrive Factors (Part I)	Score			
	Stage 1	Stage 2	Stage 3	Total
Self-Reflection				
Feedback				
Collaboration				
Student Relationships				
Inclusion				
Thrive Domains (Part II)	Score			
Classroom Community Self-Efficacy				
Instruction Self-Efficacy				
Student Engagement Self-Efficacy				
Self-Care Self-Efficacy				
Total of Thrive Domain Scores				

Self-Reflection			
Stage 1 Teacher-Focused Reflection	Stage 2 Student-Focused Reflection	Stage 3 Reflective Leadership	Total Self-Reflection Score

The results from the first part of the Thrive Inventory will help you guide your exploration through the rest of this book. The results can help determine which sections may be most germane to your set of circumstances, dispositions, and habits. These results above indicate your belief in your abilities to leverage self-reflection as a tool to enhance your teacher self-efficacy. The individual scores for stages 1, 2, and 3 will indicate your proclivity to apply self-reflection at each level.

The highest possible total score is 30. The total score is an informal measure of your reflective efficacy. In other words, this total score indicates the belief you have in your ability to leverage self-reflection to improve your practice. Consider the following scale as you reflect on your total score:

25–30: High reflective efficacy
19–24: Moderate reflective efficacy
13–18: Emerging reflective efficacy
   <13: Low reflective efficacy

Interpreting the scores for each level of self-reflection requires a little more nuance. First, consider stage 1, teacher-focused reflection. The highest possible score for each level is ten. A score of six or below indicates that teacher-focused reflection could be an area for growth and focus. A score of seven or higher indicates a belief in your ability to apply teacher-focused self-reflection.

Since each level builds upon the skills developed at the previous level, it is not likely you will have a high score at stage 2 or 3 without a high score at stage 1. In other words, it is challenging to have refined student-focused reflective skills without strong teacher-focused skills. If you did score seven or higher for stage 1, shift your focus to stage 2. You are essentially looking for the highest level at which you have a strong belief in your skills. If you scored seven or higher in stage 2, shift your consideration to stage 3. A drop in your score at any level indicates a great place to focus your self-reflection improvement efforts.

As you have surely noticed by now, this book is built around questions. Since the primary purpose is to help you map your journey toward a long and rewarding career, your thoughts are paramount. As you come across the questions throughout the following few chapters, you can use the results of these inventories to decide which questions warrant more of your time and energy. The questions are strategically placed throughout the text where they apply most directly to the aspect of the Thrive Factor being explored.

SELF-REFLECTION AND THE FOUR DOMAINS OF TEACHER SELF-EFFICACY

You previously explored the four domains of teacher self-efficacy. They include instructional self-efficacy, student engagement self-efficacy, classroom community self-efficacy, and self-care efficacy. The following five chapters about career stages of each factor address teacher self-efficacy as a whole. Having said that, the Five Thrive Factors support the four domains of teacher self-efficacy individually. The factors impact each domain based on the way you leverage the factor.

Consider the factor of self-reflection. If you focus your self-reflection on instruction, you are most likely to boost your instructional self-efficacy. If you focus your reflection on student engagement, you are most likely to boost your engagement efficacy. Although self-reflection impacts your overall teacher self-efficacy, it is essential to think deeply about improving your efficacy in each domain.

This relationship between the focus of your reflection and the impact on the most closely related domain makes intuitive sense, but it should also drive your action planning. By examining your results on the Thrive Domain portion of the inventory, you can see where your relative teacher self-efficacy strengths lie. In each chapter, you can jot down your scores to remind you where you may want to focus your energies. As you contemplate the impact self-reflection could have on your self-efficacy, keep in mind these four domains. Think about your connection between self-reflection and the four domains and use that information to guide your professional learning.

Thrive Domains (Part II)	Score
Classroom Community Self-Efficacy	
Instruction Self-Efficacy	
Student Engagement Self-Efficacy	
Self-Care Self-Efficacy	

Look back at your Thrive Domain scores. Which domain do you feel would most likely benefit from additional self-reflection? In the final chapter, you will have an opportunity to include your insight in your action planning.

STAGE 1: TEACHER-FOCUSED REFLECTION

An educator engaged in teacher-focused reflection can sustain and increase their self-efficacy. We need to remember that the earlier levels of development in all Five Thrive Factors are still valuable and are, in fact, critical. The more advanced stages do not supplant the previous stages; they supplement them. Without building the skills at the early stage of each factor, teachers cannot feasibly access the more advanced stages. Furthermore, most teachers do not reach the highest level in all five factors. It is simply not necessary. Instead, you must find the skills and pathways that you can most naturally master.

Teachers who develop student-focused reflective skills do not abandon teacher-focused reflection. On the contrary, the student focus simply enhances the reflective capacity since, ultimately, any student learning improvement will hinge upon our adult instructional decisions. Understanding this relationship will help you identify where you are on the continuum of self-reflection. With this understanding, you can identify the next steps in your self-reflection skill development. With this, you are well on your way to charting your journey to a thriving career.

CHARACTERISTICS OF TEACHER-FOCUSED REFLECTION

In this section, you will take stock of the five characteristics of teacher-focused reflection. Each of these characteristics will exist to varying degrees in any self-reflective practice. These characteristics are also interdependent. By deliberately shifting just one of these characteristics, you can often indirectly shift one or more of the others. Let us start with the most apparent characteristic.

Adult-Centric: Teacher-focused reflection is not only focused on the teacher, it is focused on teaching. In other words, teachers engaged in teacher-focused reflection are especially tuned into the act of teaching. In a cause-effect relationship, teaching is the cause and learning is the effect. This sort of reflection is aligned to the cause side of this relationship. Teacher-focused reflection typically identifies specific teaching strategies that went well or fell short of expectations. Although not exclusively, this sort of reflection tends to focus more on academics than other aspects of teaching, such as social-emotional learning.

Prioritizes Improved Instruction: Successful teacher-focused reflection results in improved instruction. Notice the product is not directly student learning. We could assume that enhanced student learning would be the natural by-product of improved instruction, but that is not the expressed purpose.

Episodic: Teacher-focused reflection tends to take place in a single episode. Once the teacher concludes their reflective thinking and decides on some future adjusted action, the cycle is complete. The episodic nature of this sort of reflection does not necessarily limit the volume of reflection, as the teacher can simply engage in a new reflective focus on some aspect of their teaching. Episodic reflection leans to a monodirectional style. The reflection serves as input that generates changes in teaching practice, but the results do not automatically trigger more reflection. One can easily identify episodic reflection by its defined beginning and end.

Reactive: Teacher-focused reflection gravitates toward a reactive posture, meaning it occurs as a direct result of some external influence. Often teachers engage in reactive reflection because something out of the ordinary or exceptional occurred during their teaching. These outstanding stimuli can be perceived as either positive or negative. For instance, a teacher may present a lesson and find the instruction fell flat and did not flow as expected. This could trigger reflection that results in a modified lesson plan for the next period. Notice that the teacher associates the perception, in this case, to the teaching, not to the students' responses.

Cooperative: One of the inherent advantages of teacher-focused reflection is that it lends itself to cooperative problem-solving. Teachers who cooperate based on reflection share their ideas about quality teaching. When teachers reflect on their teaching after an experience, they can naturally share their reflections with others. Cooperative reflection often takes place with informal gatherings of teachers discussing their experiences.

This cooperation can take place during the reflective process or after. For example, a group of teachers could meet as part of a curriculum improvement process and reflect on what has gone well in the past or where there are opportunities for improvement. In this case, the cooperation occurs during the reflection. However, a teacher may reflect on an instructional dilemma they are facing and then cooperate with a group of colleagues to identify possible solutions. In this case, the cooperation takes place after the reflection.

These characteristics can all be present to varying degrees in any reflective experience. They all exist on a continuum. We will explore these continua in more detail when we explore student-centered reflection. Now, let us spend some time dissecting examples of teacher-focused reflection to cement our understanding and set the stage to move toward more advanced forms of self-reflection.

EXAMPLES OF TEACHER-FOCUSED REFLECTION

The following scenarios represent actual teachers in the field and were collected in research-based interviews. As you read each scenario, consider each of the four domains of teacher self-efficacy. How would the reflective behaviors of each of these teachers support the four domains?

SCENARIO #1

Brianna teaches in a large suburban high school. She has been teaching English for three years. Brianna considers herself a reflective practitioner. She keeps a teaching journal in which she religiously records quick "highlights" and "lowlights" of the day. She also records "things to think about," including teaching ideas for upcoming lessons or adjustments to lessons for the following year. In addition, Brianna belongs to a teacher book club where a group of seven teachers meets twice a month to enjoy a few adult beverages as they discuss both fiction and nonfiction books related to teaching and leadership, often from the perspective of women leaders.

SCENARIO #1 ANALYSIS

- *Teaching-Centric:* It is evident in this scenario that Brianna's reflection is focused directly on her teaching, not student learning.
- *Prioritizes Improved Instruction:* Her "things to think about" reflection strategy clarifies Brianna's emphasis on future instruction.
- *Collaborative:* Brianna has found ways to enhance her self-efficacy by capitalizing on reflective collaboration in her book club.

Do you share any characteristics or habits with Brianna? Which domains would be most directly supported by Brianna's collaboration?

SCENARIO #2

Marty teaches students in sixth- through twelfth-grade science in a small rural secondary school. He is in his fifth year of teaching. He describes himself as a pragmatist. Upon first consideration, Marty did not consider himself an exceptionally reflective teacher. However, as he described his habits, he came to realize that he engages in quite a few reflective practices. Although he does not engage in any formal reflective practices such as journaling, he tends to meet with the other science teacher at least two or three times per week to plan. During these planning sessions, reflections on teaching inevitably occur. Marty also maintains a haphazard collection of sticky notes in his teacher's edition of his textbooks. He fills it with quick notes about how specific lessons went and how they could be reconsidered. In addition, Marty recently took on the responsibility of serving as a mentor, which has encouraged him to become more metacognitively aware of his teaching. The conversations with Marty's mentee often include reflections on his teaching practices to illustrate instruction and classroom engagement points.

SCENARIO # 2 ANALYSIS

- *Teaching-Centric:* Marty's reflection is clearly focused on his instruction with little emphasis on the student perspective.

- *Episodic and Reactive:* Marty engages in clearly defined episodes of reflection with his teammates. His mentoring is also episodic and reactive. Marty shares off-the-cuff examples from his teaching experience to illustrate points with his mentee. Each one of these reflective opportunities stands on its own with a defined beginning and end.
- *Prioritizes Improved Instruction:* Marty focuses on his recent and future instruction, as evidenced by the content of his conversations and his sticky-note strategy.
- *Collaborative:* Marty relies heavily on collaboration to amplify his collaboration with his colleagues and mentees.

Clearly, Marty's reflection is focused on instruction. How could Marty's reflection improve any of the domains of his teacher self-efficacy?

SCENARIO #3

Bernadette teaches students with learning disabilities in a midsize urban elementary school. She has been teaching for nine years. Bernadette considers herself a highly reflective teacher. Bernadette has a close relationship with her mother, who is also a teacher. She spends the majority of her 25-minute commute home talking with her mother about her day teaching. They discuss her instructional practices, IEP meetings, and collaboration with her general education partners. They do discuss specific students, but these conversations are primarily anecdotal and rarely result in changes in practice. Bernadette has begun to engage in meaningful reflection based on the needs of her students. The results of her reflection focus on instructional changes she can make well into the future, whether next year or the next unit of instruction.

SCENARIO #3 ANALYSIS

- *Teaching-Centric:* In this scenario, we can see Bernadette moving ever so close to a student-centric approach. However, she falls slightly short in that the adjustments are not made in real-time to benefit the students she is working with. It is important to remember that all these characteristics exist on a continuum. There is always room for movement toward a more student-centered approach.
- *Episodic:* In this example, Bernadette is still reflecting within a single episode. She cannot engage in a genuinely cyclical process because she is not adjusting her instruction on the fly. By the time she actively reflects on her teaching, she has already moved on to the next preplanned learning experience, whether next year or the next unit.
- *Reactive:* Bernadette has moved toward a less-reactive response by ritualizing her reflection. Because she chats with her mom every night, she can reflect on the

highs and lows of the ordinary days and the uncommon ones. This allows her to become more responsive since her reflection is not triggered by the extraordinary, which typically invites a more reactive response.
- *Prioritizes Improved Instruction:* Bernadette squarely aims her reflection on instructional improvements and not student learning outcomes. She plans for long-term instructional improvement that is not guaranteed to positively impact the students with whom she is currently working. Although thoughts about student interactions or responses often initiate her reflection, she wonders what she can do better next time, not what she can do better right now. Her current habits position her perfectly for advancing to the next stage in her self-reflection development.

How could Bernadette's reflection support her self-care efficacy?

All of the teachers represented in these scenarios are committed to the critical practice of self-reflection. At this point in their careers, their self-reflection gravitates toward the teacher-focused end of the continuum. We should all celebrate this sort of reflection as it sets the stage for continuous growth and refinement. This growth and refinement can lead to the self-efficacy boosting juggernaut of student-focused reflection.

STAGE 2: STUDENT-FOCUSED REFLECTION

When we engage in student-focused reflection, we simply switch perspectives. Teacher-focused reflection involves teachers thinking deeply about their practices and instruction. With student-focused reflection, we turn our attention to students and their learning. These two forms of reflection can similarly result in improved instruction. There are, however, significant differences in the manner in which the improved instruction impacts students.

We previously explored five characteristics of teacher-focused reflection. Each of these characteristics exists on a continuum. When we classify reflection as student-centered, the characteristic on the opposite end of the continuum more aptly describes the teachers' reflective habits. The section below compares each of these characteristics. In the subsequent sections, we will compare the three forms of reflection to understand student-focused reflection fully.

CHARACTERISTICS OF STUDENT-FOCUSED REFLECTION

Self-reflection boosts self-efficacy at the highest level when that reflection is squarely focused on students. This relationship stands to reason since teachers' self-efficacy is defined by their belief in their ability to meet their students' academic, social, and emotional needs. This can only be accurately measured by focusing on students and their related needs. Therefore, thriving teachers engage in student-focused reflection, which is distinguished by the following six characteristics.

Student-Centric: While engaged in student-focused reflection, teachers consider the actions, behaviors, and learning results of students as the primary source of reflective inspiration. The reflection is initiated due to student behavior, not the actions of teachers or other adults. The concerns of students dominate the conversations in student-focused reflection. Even when instructional decisions are made due to the reflection, the conversation remains focused on how this improved instruction will impact students.

Prioritizes Student Learning: Not only is student-focused reflection student-centric, it is also predominantly focused on student learning results. Teachers may focus on academic, social, emotional, or behavioral learning while engaging in student-focused reflection. With this sort of reflection, observed student learning behavior or a preplanned reflective routine triggers the initial reflection. With student-focused reflection, instructional decisions stem from the reflection on student learning, not teaching practice.

Cyclical: Student-focused reflection lends itself to cyclical reflection that can involve many iterations. As teachers reflect on student learning behaviors, they may adjust their instruction, resulting in changes in the previously observed behavior. The teacher then reflects on the new student learning behavior and adjusts their instruction, thus engaging in an entirely new reflective cycle. This sort of reflection results in continuous improvement through the refining of instructional strategies.

Multidirectional: Student-focused reflection depends on input from students. This dynamic opens opportunities for multidirectional feedback cycles to emerge. A multidirectional feedback cycle involves students providing feedback to teachers resulting in the teacher providing feedback to the student. For example, a student may provide indirect feedback indicating they do not understand a concept by sharing misconceptions in a small group. The teacher can then provide feedback to the student by helping them reflect on and rethink their misconception. This could then result in the student providing direct feedback to the teacher describing a helpful strategy. Multidirectional feedback combined with cyclical reflection can create a learning environment that naturally thrives based on the rich dialogue and feedback available to everyone.

Responsive: Student-focused feedback is responsive to student need, not reactive. Thoughtful and strategic reflection is responsive to student needs instead of an emotional and rash response to teaching that did not go as planned. By focusing on student needs, teachers reflect deeply on what the student needs. These needs are often complex and cannot be adequately addressed by a one-time adjustment to instruction. These complex needs require a teacher-student relationship based on trust and a shared commitment to success.

Collaborative: We found that teacher-focused reflection offers an opportunity for collaborative reflection with colleagues. Collaboration in student-centric reflection is also possible, if not as natural. Instructional coaches offer an excellent service to increase the possibility of collaborative student-centered reflection. Diane Sweeney's student-centered coaching model is a robust framework for instructional coaching that allows meaningful collaboration based on student-centered reflection.[1]

STAGE 3: REFLECTIVE LEADERSHIP

The most advanced stage of self-reflection is reflective leadership. Teachers who engage in reflective leadership not only focus on their students, they reflect on the students in their school, district, or beyond. In addition, these teachers find ways to leverage their reflective capacity for systemic improvement. Thriving teachers can exercise this reflective leadership from a group as small as one teaching partner or a professional learning community to as large as their entire district or beyond.

The concept of reflective leadership brings up an interesting phenomenon that impacts each of the Five Thrive Factors. Not all teachers feel comfortable accessing both sources of fuel in the Focus and Influence Model. While most thriving teachers comfortably progress through the stages on the refined focus side of the model, fewer teachers are comfortable assuming a mantle of expanding influence. Teachers are natural caregivers who can find the label of "expert" or "leader" intimidating or even offensive.

Reflective leadership, by definition, leverages expanding influence. The expanding influence of self-reflection does not need to take place on a grand stage for all to see. It can be just as impactful to teachers' self-efficacy if it takes place within a small collaborative group. Reflective leadership can serve as a comfortable entrée into the realm of expanding influence when exercised in low-risk environments such as team meetings or informal gathering of like-minded colleagues.

The following three examples of reflective leadership illustrate the scope of potential reflective leadership. Teachers are afforded ample opportunity to exercise reflective leadership in professional learning community (PLC) teams. Professional learning community structures are typical best-practice structures encouraging meaningful dialogue among teachers about student learning data.

A reflective teacher who has already transitioned from teacher-focused reflection to student-focused reflection can influence other team members to be more reflective using the tools that naturally guide the PLC process. For example, protocols are typically used as a way to structure the dialogue with the PLC team. In addition, the reflective teacher can exercise influence by asking probing questions of their teammates to increase collaborative reflection.

The PLC process is inherently fertile ground for meaningful reflection. When coupled with demonstrable student learning results, PLCs serve as teacher self-efficacy factories. Because the PLC structures are so ubiquitous and the associated best practices are commonly agreed upon, teachers can step into the role of reflective leader with relative ease.

If you crave reflective leadership beyond the scope of your teaching team, you could consider bringing your reflective skills to bear at the school and district level. Teacher voice is critical to meaningful and long-lasting school improvement. When reflective leaders serve on school or district-level teams, they naturally enhance the effectiveness of their team. Sometimes that reflection takes the form of applying a practitioner's lens to a proposed initiative. Other times, the reflective leadership takes the form of pushing back on a plan that has not been thoroughly vetted.

For instance, you may be invited to join a curriculum review team charged with the responsibility of prioritizing standards, developing curricular goals, and recommending the adoption of a resource. As a reflective leader, you could seize this opportunity to encourage a meaningful reflective practice that engages the rest of the team in moving beyond the mechanics of writing the curriculum. For example, you could ask questions that help colleagues reflect on student responses to previous learning experiences. You could then extend this reflective process by incorporating the newfound insight into the plans for the next curricular iteration. By doing this, a reflective leader can capitalize on the power of illuminating multiple perspectives.

You previously read about Angie Scioli, an extraordinary high school teacher who built excellent relationships with students. Angie is also a highly reflective educator. Eventually, her reflection compelled her to use her voice to advocate for teachers throughout her state as a founding leader of the Red4Ed movement in North Carolina. Through Red4Ed, Angie Scioli exercised the highest level of reflective leadership.

Red4Ed advocated for more teacher voice in the decision processes that impact the schools, students, and teachers of North Carolina.[2] Red4Ed has recently archived its website, meaning it is not actively generating new content. However, the following quote from their website speaks volumes to their impact and influence bolstered by reflective and dedicated teachers:

> In the fall of 2020, the Red4Ed board decided to archive this website for a variety of reasons. The most compelling reason is that it is no longer needed; members of our group now hold key leadership positions in state-level institutions, and those institutions have communication platforms with wider reach and greater influence.[3]

THE SELF-REFLECTION DEVELOPMENT PROCESS

In the previous chapter, you explored the Focus and Influence Model, which described the two forms of fuel that enable teachers to foster their self-efficacy throughout their careers. Refined focus and expanded influence propel teachers through the career progression in each of the Five Thrive Factors. Therefore, instead of sharing new scenarios of student-centered reflection, we will revisit the previous scenarios of teacher-focused reflection.

You will have the opportunity to identify the potential adjustments these teachers could make to move toward a more student-focused paradigm. Then, as you consider each vignette, put yourself in the shoes of a coach helping the teacher advance to the next level of student reflection. You will then be able to apply that same logic to your reflective habits more easily.

SCENARIO #1

Brianna was the teacher who journaled and engaged in book talks. Her reflection focused on teaching with the goal of improved instruction. Brianna has two obvious opportunities to move toward student-focused reflection. One of these opportunities would capitalize on the self-efficacy fuel of refined focus, while the other would address the influence fuel.

First, she could alter her journaling strategy. Instead of reflecting on her teaching, she could pick two or three students who demonstrate interesting learning behaviors. Examples could include challenges a student faced in a particular learning experience or assessment, or a breakthrough a student experienced with an especially challenging topic. It would be enough to switch the focus to students, but she could turn that reflection back toward her actions and plan a personalized approach to addressing the students' needs.

Second, Brianna could find ways to transform her book club into the impetus for professional growth. Brianna could identify a few student-centered opportunities for school improvement and organize professional book talks around that topic. She could create protocols for the discussion that focus the positive conversation on actual students, thus exerting her influence. What else could Brianna do to move toward student-centered self-reflection?

SCENARIO #2

Marty is a secondary science teacher who did not initially view himself as reflective. He informally engages in reflective planning with his colleagues. Marty reflects on his teaching by recording his instructional observations with sticky notes and often shares his reflections with teachers he mentors.

Mentoring presents a unique opportunity for Marty to enhance his self-reflection fueled by expanded influence. As a mentor, Marty could embrace the concept of student-centered coaching. This model emphasizes opening dialogue about student learning behavior. By encouraging others to reflect on students, he would naturally enhance his student-focused reflective capacity. What else might Marty try to become an even more student-focused reflector?

SCENARIO #3

Bernadette is the special educator who reflects with her mom every night. She is moving toward a student-focused approach but focuses on purely instructional improvements instead of student learning improvement. Bernadette could propel her self-reflection toward a student-focused approach by becoming more deliberate. By more deliberately personalizing instruction based on her reflections about her students, she could set herself up to thrive!

She has already ritualized her reflection, but she could certainly take a more student-focused approach by talking with her mom about student learning, not the success or shortcomings of her lessons. This subtle shift could open opportunities for meaningful student-focused reflection that will systematically enhance her self-efficacy. How else might Bernadette refine her focus or expand her influence?

CHARTING YOUR SELF-REFLECTION PATHWAY

How can you take what you have learned and develop some actionable goals to refine your self-reflective skills? Your path toward more meaningful teacher self-reflection is unique. What works for one teacher will not necessarily work for another. The best path for you is one that builds on your natural reflective strengths and capitalizes on your existing reflective habits. You can use your results from the Thrive Inventory to formulate a self-reflection baseline from which to work.

- Based on what you have read and your results from the Thrive Inventory, how would you describe your level of self-reflection?
- Do you gravitate toward teacher-focused reflection, student-focused reflection, reflective leadership, or a combination?
- Where would you like to enhance your self-reflective skills?
- Which of the four teacher self-efficacy domains do you feel could be supported by your self-reflection? How?

As you consider the progression from one level to the next on the self-reflection continuum, keep in mind the Focus and Influence Model you read about in the previous chapter. This model explains that the path from one level to the next in any of the Five Thrive Factors is fueled by a refined focus on students or expanding influence. As we will see in the following sections, both focus and influence can propel the progression from each level to the next, but in some cases, one of the fuel sources is more evident and direct. If you do not mind writing in your book, jot down your Thrive Inventory score next to each self-reflection career progression level.

ENHANCING TEACHER-FOCUSED REFLECTION

As described in the Focus and Influence Model, the first step on the influence ladder is influence on self. Influence on self is based on the most basic level of self-efficacy. You must believe in your capacity to change and grow to build self-efficacy. Similarly, the first rung on the refined focus ladder focuses on self. For example, when you are trying to build your teacher-focused reflective skills, you need to turn your focus inward and rely on your reserve of reflective capacity to change your habits of reflection deliberately.

Not all of us are naturally reflective. If this is the case, just developing some reflective habits can go a long way toward boosting your self-efficacy. The easiest way to start is to focus on your teaching and schedule a specific time to engage in the reflection. When can you carve out five to ten minutes to pump the brakes on your busy day and just think about the effectiveness of your teaching?

It is vital to keep the time frame short. If you set unrealistic goals, you are much less likely to succeed. A drive home, a morning walk, or even a few minutes of your prep time all can satisfy the need for a bit of reflection time. Ask yourself these two fundamental questions:

1. What went well today, and how did I contribute to it going well?
2. What might I do differently next time?

As you respond to these questions, avoid self-criticism. If you are reflection averse, it is quite likely that you may be apprehensive about criticism. Self-criticism can be one of the most insidious forms. Therefore, this level of self-reflection skill-building should be as positive as possible.

It is essential to consider the mechanics of the habits of reflection. Will you use a journal, or will you simply think? Are you more likely to be successful if you reflect at school, at home, or someplace else? Would you benefit from a reflective partner such as a coach or teacher friend? Once you have answered these questions, set a goal. Following the SMART Goal formula is always a great option. SMART is an acronym for the five qualities of a vital goal:

- **S**—Specific: What do you hope to accomplish? Be crystal clear.
- **M**—Measurable: How will you know you have accomplished it? What is the scale for success?
- **A**—Achievable: Set the bar high enough to inspire but not so high as to intimidate.
- **R**—Relevant: Make sure your goal is aligned with your core principles. Make it matter.
- **T**—Time bound: When will you accomplish this goal?

A stage 1 self-reflection goal might read as follows: I will improve my reflective capacity by reflecting on my two key questions regarding how to be more present with my students four out of five days on my drive home.

Give it a try and write your own SMART goal about self-reflection!

MOVING FROM TEACHER-FOCUSED TO STUDENT-FOCUSED REFLECTION

To move from teacher-focused to student-focused reflection, you must identify your barriers. It is critical to acknowledge that there is a reason teachers typically progress through these stages in order as they progress through their careers. Experience supports reflection. If you are a relatively new teacher, give yourself some grace and be patient. If you are motivated to improve your reflective capacity, you will!

The shift toward student-focused reflection is fueled primarily by refined focus. At this point in the progression of self-reflection, you must invert the bulk of your focus from an intrapersonal lens to an interpersonal lens. Instead, you must shift your focus to students and their learning behaviors.

Background knowledge and experience allow teachers to nimbly reflect by accessing that prior knowledge through reflection and quickly adjusting their course. You can accelerate this development through intentionality. Instead of passively letting the process of developing a student-focused reflective lens occur with time, make a plan and execute that plan.

You can increase intentionality by shifting your habits. Metacognition refers to our ability to think about our thinking. As you are reflecting, slow down and deeply analyze what you are thinking about. Do your best to focus on students and their learning behaviors. When you feel yourself drifting too quickly to a focus on your teaching, name the behavior and shift. You might have a self-talk phrase you rely on to shift to maintain the student focus.

Shifting your prompting question will accelerate your development as well. Ask questions about students.

- Which students had learning breakthroughs today?
- Who is a student who struggled with a concept today? What was the specific challenge?
- Which students could use more support socially and emotionally?

Indeed, each of these questions will, at some point, require a follow-up question asking what you are going to do to address the identified issues. The trick is to fight this urge long enough to know that you have developed an empathetic view of the students' perspective. At its highest level, student-focused reflection results in you cognitively walking in the students' shoes. In this way, you can ensure your teaching responses are as aligned to their needs as possible.

Student-focused reflection allows for the reflection-in-action we explored earlier. Reflection-in-action takes place while you are teaching and allows for micro-adjustments laser-focused on individual needs. You can build these skills by planning for them. Small formative assessments can give you the data you need to reflect and adjust quickly. You must give yourself time. You can build your two-minute reflection opportunities right into your lesson plans until you build the automaticity allowing an authentic student-focused reflection habit to develop.

MOVING TOWARD REFLECTIVE LEADERSHIP

Moving toward reflective leadership leans more heavily on the expanding influence ladder of the Focus and Influence Model. Reflective leadership is defined by an expanding influence. If you are ready for this step, you are probably finding yourself yearning for opportunities to contribute to the improvement of your school or district. You likely feel like you have more to give. Good for you! Our schools need more courageous leaders.

If you are ready and interested in bolstering your reflective leadership skills, there are certain habits you can deliberately develop. First, you can hone your observation skills. By more critically observing your surroundings, you can uncover opportunities for reflective leadership. For example, you could observe your behaviors and the behaviors of team members during a meeting and compare those behaviors to the norms you have established.

Second, you can practice dispassionate reflection. Dispassion does not mean you should not care; it describes being rational and impartial. By being dispassionate, you resist the influence for overstated emotions. For example, you could come home from a hard day and journal about what made the day hard instead of venting on Facebook only to be potentially triggered by the responses of others.

Finally, you can practice being open-minded. We live in a world where strong opinions not necessarily based on fact or reason often rule the day. Even in this environment, you can enhance your reflective skills by listening to understand, even if you will never agree. Not only do these characteristics describe high-quality reflection but they also light the path toward reflective leadership. By observing, exercising dispassion, and remaining open to the ideas of others, you position yourself to be a highly impactful reflective leader.

As a reflective leader, your first job is to simultaneously reflect on your students, your actions as a teacher, and the actions of your colleagues. For example, how often do you notice a colleague engaged in a practice that may benefit from some reflection and refinement? This simple question sets in motion the opportunity to expand your influence by naming and noticing the behavior you observed.

Sometimes your colleague may seek your reflective talents; other times, you may lean in on your own accord. Either way, relying on the ability to ask great questions is your greatest asset. How equipped do you feel to step into that conversation without being perceived as patronizing or out of line? This is a pivotal moment for many teachers who dip their toes in the water of reflective coaching. It can be tricky.

By asking open-ended questions free from judgment, you increase the likelihood that your colleagues will welcome your support. Crafting judgment-free questions sounds easier than it is. However, simply asking open-ended questions does not mean they are devoid of judgment. We have all had the coworker who asks an "open-ended" question that, in their mind, has a correct answer. Therefore, it is critical that you are authentically curious about the responses and perspectives of your colleagues.

Questions beginning with "why" are a great place to start as they get to intention and the core of decision-making. The "five-why" method of root-cause analysis is an excellent strategy for enhancing understanding. In short, this method involves asking a series of "why-based" questions of an individual until you both agree you have dug deeply enough to have uncovered the reason behind decisions. Here is an example of a five-why exchange between a coach and teacher:

> Coach: In looking at this math assessment data, it appears that questions 7–11 were particularly difficult for a portion of your class. Why do you think this might be the case?
>
> Teacher: Oh, those are story problems. I have a group of kids who consistently struggle with those.
>
> Coach: Why do you think they struggle with them?
>
> Teacher: Well, those questions have a lot of extra language that trips them up. I am pretty sure they get the math concept.
>
> Coach: Why does the extra language trip up some and not others?
>
> Teacher: Well, let me see. Oh . . . three of the struggling kids are English language learners, and two of the others tend not to engage very deeply in our small-group conversations.
>
> Coach: Why are the students who are English language learners struggling with the story problems?
>
> Teacher: Well, they don't spend a lot of cognitive energy decoding the words. Figuring out if the words are important or not is another skill altogether.
>
> Coach: I think we are on to something. How do you think you could support them?

There is no magic in the number five. Continue with the questions until clarity emerges. In this example, the coach asked four "why" questions and then transitioned into a "how" to get to the next steps. Consider this word of caution when using the five-why technique: make sure you are not perceived as an interrogator. This technique can go badly if mutual trust has not been established. If it has, the "five whys" can work wonders.

COACHES CORNER

In the "Coaches Corner" sections, you have an opportunity to switch perspectives and explore ways to support others on their journey toward a thriving and efficacious career.

Thus far, we have approached our exploration of teacher self-efficacy from the teacher perspective. Coaching serves as critical support for teachers as they strive to improve their self-efficacy and refine their practice to ensure continuous growth. Thriving veteran teachers benefit from coaching conversations just as much as novice teachers. This coaching can occur with a principal, an instructional coach, or any instructional leader with the skill to engage in meaningful dialogue about teaching and learning.

We will examine the ways coaching contributes to each of the Five Thrive Factors. In these "Coaches Corners," you will find practical strategies to help your colleagues thrive. These same strategies may help you find greater success as you work with coaches, principals, or other instructional leaders. Each strategy is accompanied by precisely aligned tools such as protocols, inventories, and rubrics.

Self-reflection flourishes with the support of coaching. Effective coaching requires reflection on the part of the coachee. Coaches focus their efforts on encouraging the teachers with whom they work to think deeply about their instructional dilemmas and uncover their solutions. This formula applies to any instructional leader who depends on coaching as a tool for professional growth.

Indeed, any of the tools described in this book can be used by a coach to support teachers. For example, the following is one activity a coach could use to activate some neurons and dendrites. A coach could follow these steps to help teachers develop self-awareness when it comes to teacher-focused or student-focused reflection:

- Get five sticky notes and a pen.
- Take a moment to stop and think about how your last school day went.
- Quickly write down the first five short phrases or sentences that come to mind describing your day.
- Sort the Post-it notes into two groups.
- One group represents descriptors that are primarily related to students (i.e., my first guided reading group knocked it out of the park; Charise emerged as a leader; or Tony seems to be struggling to maintain his friendships).
- The other group represents descriptors primarily related to you or other adults (i.e., my lesson on Civil Rights was great!; Mr. Delacruz really helped Charise come out of her shell; or My friendship lesson in Morning Meeting was a flop!).

This very nonscientific experiment will help you identify if your tendencies lean toward teacher-focused or student-focused reflection. Now consider the following questions:

- Did you have all your sticky notes in one column?
- If not, which column had more?
- How does this distribution relate to your perception of your reflective tendencies?
- How could you adjust any of the teacher-focused comments to be more student-centered?
- How did or could your student-focused reflections improve your practice?

The best coaching relies on eliciting the thoughts, opinions, and conclusions of the teacher being coached. Reflection is the path to illuminate these emerging thoughts. Whether you are a mentor, instructional coach, or principal, specific tools to encourage meaningful reflection can prove highly beneficial. This coaching tool is an excellent place to start.

CHAPTER REFLECTIONS

1. How would you describe your reflective habits?
2. Has how you reflect changed in any way since you began your career?
3. Do you reflect on your professional and personal life? Which do you do more? Why?
4. Are you aware you are reflecting when you reflect?
5. What conditions make it easier for you to engage in meaningful reflection?

ACTION PLAN

At the end of this and the four subsequent chapters, you will have the opportunity to articulate goals and an actionable next step related to each of the Five Thrive Factors. However, before we engage in the action planning for self-reflection, take a moment to consider your vision for yourself as an educator. Thriving is about becoming, not being. You are continually growing, learning, and expanding your ability to impact your students positively.

This next question for you is both the most simple and most complex in this book. Who do you want to become as a teacher? This question is about identity, not behavior. Take some time to reflect on this idea and jot it down in a journal, on the book's inside cover, or on a sticky note on your laptop. Most importantly, hold on to it in your heart.

Now think about the self-reflection factor. How can you use self-reflection to thrive and to move toward your vision for you? It might be a SMART goal moving you toward student-focused reflection. It might be journaling about your teaching. It might be hanging out more with your colleagues after work on a Friday even though you are exhausted because you know they have great conversations about teaching and learning. This is your journey. Where do you want to go? Once again, it is your turn to pledge to take a simple action step to get you moving in the right direction. Do not hesitate. Do not procrastinate. Just take that first step.

8
Feedback Career Stages

Travel broadens our perspectives. Travel helps us become flexible, trust the world, trust ourselves, and challenge ourselves. Through travel, we are naturally urged and nudged toward a more inclusive understanding of the world we share. Through these myriad experiences we enjoy while traveling, we receive feedback about our understandings and biases.

Travel is a positive and inspirational way to naturally (and often subconsciously) absorb feedback and grow. Have you ever returned from a trip, and you saw something differently or understood someone more completely upon reengaging in your routines? If so, this was likely encouraged by the feedback you received about your existing perspectives while traveling.

In chapter 3, we explored feedback and found that it profoundly impacts teachers' self-efficacy development. Feedback is essentially information that provides teachers an outside observer's perspective, which can translate to action. Feedback feeds the previously explored factor of self-reflection. Teachers can metacognitively reflect on their internal thoughts and observations. By harnessing the power of feedback, however, teachers can reflect on the perspectives of others.

The career development path of feedback for teachers with high self-efficacy is unique among the Five Thrive Factors. The primary distinction is that teachers receive more formal feedback in the earliest stages of their careers. Preservice teacher preparation programs prioritize feedback as a professional development tactic. New teachers often receive mentors who provide systematic feedback. This feedback is, of course, not always invited or welcomed. More on that later.

High self-efficacy teachers seek feedback as they crave information from outside sources to inform and refine their practice. Feedback, at its core, is information. It allows the receiver to see themselves and this definition certainly applies to teachers in all stages of their careers. As you will learn throughout this chapter, there is no one-size-fits-all approach to effectively leveraging feedback to support teacher self-efficacy.

As thriving teachers progress through their careers, the manner in which they seek feedback shifts. This shift primarily follows the focus side of the Focus and Influence

Model. In the earliest stages of a career, teachers rely on feedback from authority figures to bolster their self-efficacy. As they improve their ability to invite, welcome, and reflect on feedback from authority figures, they shift to a reliance on feedback from trusted peers. At the most advanced stage, thriving teachers rely on feedback directly from their students.

Unlike self-reflection, teachers can definitely receive feedback related to any of the four domains of teacher self-efficacy. Typically, however, feedback supports engagement, instructional, and classroom community self-efficacy. However, as we continue to learn more about the importance of self-care efficacy, this may change.

FEEDBACK AND THE FOUR DOMAINS OF TEACHER SELF-EFFICACY

Once again, it is time to explore the four domains of teacher self-efficacy. Take a look at the factor of feedback. If you focus your self-reflection on instruction, you are most likely to boost your instructional self-efficacy. If you focus your feedback on student engagement, you are most likely to boost your engagement efficacy. Although feedback impacts your overall teacher self-efficacy, it is essential to think deeply about improving your efficacy in each domain.

This relationship between the focus of your feedback and the impact on the most closely related domain makes intuitive sense, but it should also drive your action planning. By examining your results on the Thrive Domain portion of the inventory, you can get a sense of where your relative teacher self-efficacy strengths lie. In each chapter, you can jot down your scores as a reminder of where you may want to focus your energies. As you contemplate the impact feedback could have on your self-efficacy, keep in mind these four domains. Think about your connection between self-reflection and the four domains and use that information to guide your professional learning.

As you can see, this progression has teachers continually increasing their focus on students as they navigate their self-efficacy journeys. In this chapter, you will explore the characteristics of each of the feedback stages. You will have the opportunity to reflect on examples of each of these stages in action. Finally, chart your course toward increasing your ability to fuel your self-efficacy with feedback.

Characteristics of the Career Stages of Seeking and Valuing Feedback		
From Authority Figures	**From Peers**	**From Students**
Power Differential	Equal Power	Empowering Students
Evaluative	Nonevaluative	Nonevaluative
One-way	Collaborative	Cyclical
Formal	Informal	Formal or Informal
Indirect Impact on Students	Indirect Impact on Students	Direct Impact on Students

It is once again time to pause and reflect on the results of your Thriving Teacher Inventory. Remember that these results are not evaluative, nor are they scientific. Instead, they are designed to inspire self-reflection and activate schema as you explore each of the Five Thrive Factors. First, complete the table below with the corresponding results from the inventory. You can now use the results to maximize the impact of your reflection.

Feedback			
Stage 1 From Authority Figures	Stage 2 From Peers	Stage 3 From Students	Total Feedback Score

Consider the following scale as you reflect on your total score:

25–30: High feedback efficacy
19–24: Moderate feedback efficacy
13–18: Emerging feedback efficacy
 <13: Low feedback efficacy

Interpreting the scores for each level of feedback requires a different approach. First, think about and reflect on the first stage, feedback from authority figures. The highest possible score for each stage is ten. A score of six or below indicates that teacher-focused reflection could be an area for growth and focus. A score of seven or higher indicates a belief in your ability to leverage feedback from authority figures. These results will help illuminate your personalized path.

STAGE 1: FEEDBACK FROM AUTHORITY FIGURES

At the earliest stage, teachers lean heavily on authority figures to provide feedback. This feedback builds self-efficacy by ensuring novice teachers that they are making good choices ultimately benefiting their students. Receiving actionable and thoughtful feedback from authority figures is critical as it serves as a calibrating rudder allowing teachers to learn about valued best practices and the culture of the school.

Authority figures are defined by their relationship with the teacher with whom they work. As long as the teacher views the individual offering the feedback as someone with formal or informal authority to evaluate performance, they are authority figures. Authority figures include preservice supervisors, principals, mentors, coaches, and esteemed colleagues. The process of receiving feedback from authority figures is unique in that it can be either invited or mandated. The self-efficacy benefits of receiving feedback lie in the way teachers seek and value the feedback. This is especially so when that feedback may not have been invited.

Back in chapter 3, we explored the characteristics of effective teacher feedback. We found that the most impactful feedback teachers receive is thought-provoking, specific, and actionable. This chapter will see how those characteristics apply to each of the three stages of the feedback factor.

CHARACTERISTICS OF FEEDBACK FROM AUTHORITY FIGURES

Feedback from authority figures comes from multiple sources and in various forms. All three career stages of feedback are defined by the relationship between the giver and receiver of the feedback. An authority figure is defined as someone who is perceived as possessing power and who has the expressed responsibility to officially measure and report on teachers' performance.

Feedback from authority figures can come from formal or informal sources. Formal sources include principals, district administrators, university supervisors, or formal mentors. Informal sources could include instructional coaches, teaching colleagues who have perceived power, parents of students, or informal mentors. Regardless of where it comes from, the following characteristics define feedback from authority figures.

Power differential: A power differential always exists when feedback is offered from an authority figure. This is neither good nor bad; it just is. Regardless of their job in a school, teachers will have someone who has more institutional power than they do. Formal job responsibilities as with a principal or informal cultural power like that of a respected veteran teacher can form the basis for this power differential.

It is critical to learn to accept and value feedback. By learning how to seek out and find value in feedback from authority figures, we can break down barriers between stakeholders with various levels of institutional power. These barriers can negatively impact the potential of both the teacher and the authority figure.

From the teachers' perspective, the power of authority figures can be intimidating, causing a desire to avoid feedback. Teachers might feel the feedback is going to be overly critical and painful. Once a pattern of avoiding feedback has been established, it can be exceedingly hard to break, causing a permanent erosion of the self-efficacy boosting power of feedback. The intimidation and fear associated with receiving feedback from authority figures can come from two very different emotional perspectives.

Sometimes, teachers may hold an authority figure in such esteem that they avoid feedback out of fear of exposing their vulnerabilities. The last thing a new teacher wants is for their highly respected principal to believe they are incompetent and require extra attention. This could be especially challenging if the preservice experience for a new teacher did not offer support in the fine art of accepting feedback.

Other times, teachers may fear feedback for a very different reason. For example, if a teacher's experience with feedback from authority figures was ever demeaning or disrespectful, opening up to more feedback will be difficult. Worse yet, if a teacher's principal weaponizes feedback to drive a personal agenda or to enhance their own self-worth, the path to constructive feedback is barred. This, fortunately, is incredibly rare.

Most principals want to offer meaningful feedback to their teachers. They want to learn to improve their ability to continually offer the best possible feedback. Being a principal can be an isolating job. Offering valued feedback is one of the most direct ways a principal can serve as an instructional leader. Remember, principals and other administrators were teachers too. They do not want the power differential to get in the way of their desire to help teachers improve their craft.

Evaluative: Feedback from an authority figure naturally contains an element of evaluation. For the sake of this exploration, evaluative means that the feedback provided is linked to data included in the formal or informal summation of a teacher's effectiveness. Sometimes this evaluation is real, other times teachers simply perceive it. The perception of feedback being evaluative is accurate when the person providing the feedback has responsibility for supervising the teacher, and the feedback provided is somehow linked to the appraisal process. It is perceived when the teachers feel, accurately or not, that the feedback will find its way into their formal evaluations.

Most teacher evaluation systems appropriately rely heavily on the power of feedback as the cornerstone of the process. Research strongly supports the fact that feedback is necessary for teachers to grow. Unfortunately, the feedback's potential impact on formal evaluation systems is drastically limited because principals may have as many as forty direct reports requiring formal feedback. There is simply no way for a principal to provide meaningful and personalized feedback to this many teachers.

Principals who possess the coveted skills of expert feedback-providers ensure the bulk of their feedback is formative. These principals are typically very deliberate regarding the way they offer feedback. Additionally, before they begin providing feedback, they build relationships with teachers to generate trust in a mutual understanding that they are on the same team, both advocating for the learning of all students.

One-way: Feedback from an authority figure typically travels in only one direction. The feedback is provided from the authority figure, received by the teacher, and the process stops in its tracks right there. This is a common complaint among teachers who feel they do not have an opportunity to engage in meaningful conversations with those who evaluate them. They are rarely allowed to provide feedback *about* the feedback they receive.

Picture a typical end-of-year summative evaluation conference between a new teacher and their principal. In this setting, the principal provides feedback to summarize the teacher's effectiveness throughout the first three years. The principal focuses their energy on providing ample evidence to support their final rating while the new teacher does their best to receive the information and learn from it. There is extraordinarily little space in this sort of conversation for a cyclical exchange of feedback followed by feedback *about* the feedback

Even in a less-structured exchanges of feedback from an authority figure to teachers, challenges can arise. It can be exceedingly difficult for the teacher to engage in conversations like these with anything less than total agreement. This gets back to the point that even if the conversation is not formally evaluative, novice teachers can feel they are constantly being evaluated during every exchange they have with an authority figure.

Formal: Feedback from an authority figure often feels more formal to the teacher than feedback from peers or students. Indeed, not all feedback from an authority figure takes place exclusively in a formal evaluation process. Nevertheless, it still can be difficult for teachers to let their guards down and appreciate the feedback for what it is and how it might inform the next steps in their professional learning.

A skilled principal can sense when teachers' dialogue becomes stilted while receiving feedback. These principals can make adjustments to make the process seem less formal. Unfortunately, sometimes a principal will respond to this stilted exchange by becoming more formal to match the tenor of the conversation. Worse yet, a principal might subconsciously avoid informal exchanges and opportunities to provide feedback because they sense it has not been received well.

Indirect Impact on Students: Feedback from an authority figure generally supports an indirect impact on students. This indirect impact is not a criticism of this sort of feedback. It is simply limited by the relationship between the giver and receiver of the feedback. Teachers process the feedback from authority figures from several perspectives. They must process who is offering feedback and why they are offering it. They then process the feedback as it relates to their evaluation. It is more difficult to internalize the feedback if it is associated with a formal rating.

These perspectives are uniquely associated with feedback from an authority figure and can result in the feedback being overly simplified and classified as positive or negative. This binary dynamic mitigates impact by thwarting self-reflection and encouraging a simple checkbox mentality of classifying the teaching practice as good or bad.

This limiting perspective is the primary factor that mitigates the impact on students. This sort of feedback becomes hyper-focused on what the teacher is doing. Even if the feedback provider offers student-focused feedback, the teacher looks inward and considers the feedback from the evaluator's perspective. Thoughts like, "I wonder what she thinks of this?"; "I hope this is good enough for him"; or "I really wish she wouldn't have seen that" get in the way of focusing more directly on student learning.

EXAMPLES OF FEEDBACK FROM AUTHORITY FIGURES

Here are some examples of feedback from authority figures in action. Even though this feedback style relies most heavily upon the earliest stages of teachers' careers, all teachers should look for ways to improve the benefit of feedback from authority figures. Like it or not, you will always have someone responsible for providing feedback. It is up to you to find ways to maximize the impact on your practice. It is worth remembering that you can always provide feedback to your supervisor about how you prefer feedback. Whether you have engaged directly in this sort of feedback or it presents something to aspire to, visualize which examples best fit your individual feedback style preferences:

- A formal observation from a principal
- A planning session with an instructional coach
- A summative conference at the end of the school year
- Written feedback from a professor
- A casual pop-in in which your principal provides advice about your classroom community development practices
- A mentor teacher suggesting next steps in your professional development
- A principal telling you she believes you would be a great administrator

These are all forms of feedback from authority figures. You may have had an emotional response when picturing yourself receiving this sort of feedback. Feedback can be both challenging to give and to receive. Do your best to receive feedback from an authority figure with an open mind and open heart. We are all in this together and certainly want what is best for our students.

STAGE 2: FEEDBACK FROM PEERS

Many teachers who refine their skills in accepting feedback from authority figures learn to rely on feedback to support their self-efficacy. As they look to maximize their impact, evaluative feedback from authority figures proves to be insufficient. The next step in the progression thriving teachers take is to turn to peers as a source of meaningful feedback.

We must take a moment to understand what we mean by the term "peer." Being one's peer is not strictly defined as having similar positions in the organization. Being a peer involves equity of voice and perspective. If you work with a teacher with more experience, more political capital, and a dominant voice that squelches your ability to be heard, they are not your peer. As you will learn in this section, receiving feedback from peers can be a rewarding experience that increases the efficacy of all involved.

CHARACTERISTICS OF FEEDBACK FROM PEERS

The second career stage in the feedback process finds teachers shifting their focus from feedback from authority figures to feedback from peers. The distinction between feedback from authority figures versus peers requires an examination of the relationship between the giver and the receiver of the feedback, not just their titles. The feedback receiver is essentially the only person who can classify the feedback's giver as a peer. We can further develop an understanding of feedback from peers by exploring the following characteristics.

Equal power: If you have ever had a respected colleague share focused and insightful feedback inspiring you to adjust your instruction, you have experienced the power of feedback from peers. Feedback from peers fundamentally exists on an equal playing field. Teachers can only truly capitalize on the impact of receiving feedback if they feel comfortable being vulnerable.

If teachers perceive a power differential, they are far less likely to open themselves up with the vulnerability necessary to achieve the breakthroughs that are possible when reflecting on the feedback from peers. These breakthroughs occur when teachers drop their defenses, abandon the fear of being judged, and welcome improvement opportunities.

For instance, a teacher may open up about a difficult day with a challenging student with a trusted colleague and share their response to the student's misbehavior. The trusted colleague may recognize a blind spot of which her colleague is not aware. After acknowledging how difficult this must have been, the colleague could ask if her friend is open to feedback. Teachers willing to drop their defenses against constructive feedback allow themselves to receive the gift of a fresh perspective. This same scenario would not be as impactful if the teacher perceived a power differential.

Nonevaluative: The most formal power differential teachers can face is one which is evaluative. Teachers are not receiving feedback from a peer if the individual holds any evaluative responsibility in the relationship. This is why experts in the field of instructional coaching like Jim Knight adamantly oppose having instructional coaches involved in the formal evaluation of teachers.

If the evaluative nature of the relationship is informal, it can be more challenging to discern. For instance, a new teacher may have a mentor who provides feedback after a scheduled observation. If the teacher assumes the principal receives a report, the teacher will not receive the feedback the same way they would if they were confident the observation was confidential. Feedback from peers depends on trust. This trust can be built through consistency, honesty, and clarity.

Indirect Impact on Student: Feedback from peers can generate transformative shifts in instructional practice. Having said that, it still indirectly impacts student learning. Remember, indirect is not a criticism as all professional learning merely indirectly impacts student learning. The impact is classified as indirect because the teacher must translate the feedback into improved instruction, potentially improving student learning outcomes.

However, feedback from peers removes some barriers to improving student learning that may influence feedback received from authority figures. First, because feedback from peers is based on a trusting relationship, the feedback is easier to hear and internalize. Once the feedback is internalized, the teacher can more readily adjust their instruction.

Collaborative: When peers work together toward a common goal, they unlock the potential of a truly collaborative endeavor. Collaborative feedback relies on an exchange of ideas between at least two parties. When the lines between givers and receivers of feedback are blurred, a natural dialogue focused on improved instructional practices results in a significant and enduring change.

Collaborative feedback motivates teachers to continue their work together, as it satisfies social as well as professional needs. Teachers who engage in collaborative peer-to-peer feedback tend to seek it out more and more until it becomes an integral part of their professional learning arsenal. When teachers are driven to seek opportunities to engage in peer-to-peer feedback continually, they hone their skills, which may also improve their ability to accept feedback from authority figures. It can also set them up to transition to the most advanced stage of seeking and valuing feedback from students—more on that later.

Informal: Feedback from peers is almost always informal. There are very few formal structures that rely on peer-to-peer feedback. As soon as formal structures are put in place, a power imbalance emerges, and the process reverts to feedback from authority figures. For example, a new teacher might work with a colleague down the hall and receive informal feedback regularly. If the teacher who offers the feedback transitions to the role of instructional coach, that same feedback no longer comes from a peer but from an authority figure.

Herein lies the most significant challenge with leveraging feedback from peers. Teachers must actively seek out this sort of feedback on their own. This can be especially challenging for a new teacher who may not yet have developed relationships with their colleagues allowing for this sort of professional learning. This is why most teachers do not develop the skills to capitalize on feedback from peers until they get a few years of experience under their belts.

EXAMPLES OF FEEDBACK FROM PEERS

Here are some examples of peer feedback in action. Look for yourself in these examples. Whether you have engaged directly in this sort of feedback or they present something to aspire to, visualize what this would look like in your current professional setting:

- Inviting a teaching colleague into your classroom to observe a lesson and provide feedback
- Meeting with a group of teachers regularly to share dilemmas and successes while providing feedback

- Calling a colleague on the drive home and explaining a situation and asking what they think about the choices you made
- Dedicating time in a PLC to discuss instructional decisions and specifically offer feedback on those choices
- Having a teacher colleague read your feedback to students and provide feedback about your feedback
- Co-constructing a rubric about a particular teaching practice and applying it to video-recorded lessons

The list could go on and on. The key is to find someone with whom you share trust and comfort and begin practicing the art of giving and receiving effective feedback. For more information on the qualities of effective feedback, refer to chapter 3.

STAGE 3: FEEDBACK FROM STUDENTS

The most advanced stage of seeking and valuing feedback comes directly from students. Experienced, thriving teachers learn to receive feedback directly from their students. Student assessment, of course, serves as a form of feedback from students. Highly skilled teachers, however, develop strategies to amplify the impact of receiving feedback directly from students.

Students provide direct and impactful feedback to teachers in several ways. Three means of receiving student feedback include direct verbal feedback, nonverbal feedback such as body language and affective responses, and data-based feedback such as assessment or survey results. All three of these methods of collecting feedback directly from students rely on mutual trust, empathy, and active listening. The characteristics of feedback from students paint a picture of a dynamic and student-centered learning environment facilitated by a thriving and experienced teacher.

CHARACTERISTICS OF FEEDBACK FROM STUDENTS

The highest stage in the seeking and valuing feedback career path is leveraging feedback directly from students to inform your practice. Valuing feedback from students is not only a gift to you and your practice, it is a gift to the students as it sends a strong signal that they matter to you. We will explore the five characteristics that define feedback from students. Feedback from students is empowering, nonevaluative, directly impacting students, cyclical, and can be either formal or informal.

Empowering students: In the other two career stages of feedback development, the power relationship existed between two adults. Seeking feedback from students turns this dynamic on its head. It empowers students directly by helping them develop agency in their learning. Student agency is a way of describing a student's ability to drive their learning. It is marked by relevancy, impact, and choice. A student whose teachers skillfully listen and respond to the feedback can drive their learning in a much more meaningful way than simply self-selecting learning experiences.

By asking a student about your teaching, you demonstrate an authentic vulnerability that lets your entire class know their learning is your top priority. You send messages that their opinions matter and that you are willing to adjust your practice based on their ideas. You are also empowering students by teaching them how to offer meaningful feedback. Students are often the recipients of feedback, but rarely are they allowed to give feedback in such a meaningful way.

Nonevaluative: Feedback from students is completely nonevaluative. The beauty of this sort of feedback is that it resides entirely outside of any formal evaluation process. Even though it is less common than the other forms of feedback, it is the most natural in that it exists between the two most important stakeholders in the teaching and learning process, the teacher and the student. If you embrace this natural quality of this sort of feedback, you can ensure that it does not feel evaluative.

Could a student share feedback that sounds and feels evaluative? Certainly! This simply presents an opportunity for more student learning. You could capitalize on such a situation by teaching your student how to more skillfully offer feedback that is not evaluative. In addition to this, you can simply recognize that the student does not operate within the formal chain of command and holds no evaluative authority. This would not stop you from taking a risk and asking your students to rate your teaching against a co-constructed rubric.

Direct Impact on Students: Feedback from students directly and profoundly impacts student learning. Seeking and valuing feedback from your students can be truly transformative in the learning process. This sort of feedback removes all of the barriers that mitigate the power of effective feedback. Feedback from students allows the most important stakeholders in the teaching and learning process, our students, the opportunity to provide constructive feedback to the person who holds the most potential of impacting their learning—you.

Cyclical: Teachers who regularly seek feedback from their students can engage in a cyclical process in which they are constantly analyzing and responding to the information they gather from their students. This sort of feedback falls into the category of what is often referred to as short-cycle feedback. Cyclical feedback simply means the lag time between receiving feedback and adjusting practices has been shrunk down or wholly eliminated.

By implementing short-cycle feedback processes, you can engage in many more iterations of the feedback loop, with each iteration offering a new opportunity for student-centered improvement. For instance, you could start by gathering feedback about your instruction from the whole class by conducting a quick formative assessment. Based on that formative assessment, you could create small groups to focus on individual skills needing to be honed and refined. During that small group instruction, you could gather feedback by periodically asking students which form of instruction seems to be resonating with them.

Finally, you could transition to working with one student who still requires additional instruction to master the skill. During the instruction, you could consistently check for understanding by asking the student questions to encourage metacognition. These iterations of gathering feedback from students can occur in this whole group individually, but it is unnecessary. You could just as readily gather regular feedback from all your students and adjust whole group instruction. The key is to commit to demonstrating the value of student feedback and practice, practice, practice.

Formal or Informal: Teachers can approach the practice of gathering feedback from students formally or informally. Formal practices tend to fall into the assessment category, while informal practices lean more toward active listening. For example, the formal practice of gathering student feedback would be implementing a pretesting process at the beginning of each unit. An informal practice would be periodically asking students if they understand a particular concept in the unit.

The distinction of formal versus informal is based on the process employed, and the type of information gathered from the feedback. In our examples above, the more formal process was planned and took place at the beginning of each unit. Additionally, the teacher records specific feedback about student learning to inform their instruction. In the informal example, the teacher decides when and where to seek feedback from their students. It could be based on intuition or indications of misconceptions among the students. The teacher is not recording any information but instead responding by adjusting instruction on the spot.

Teachers can maximize the benefits of gathering feedback from students by combining both informal and formal practices. It is easiest to start where you are most comfortable, develop strong habits, and then expand toward the style that may be outside your comfort zone. For example, you may be very comfortable periodically gathering feedback from students using a fist-to-five technique, which we will explore in our next section.

If this is the case, you can set a goal of using this technique three times a day for two weeks. Once you have established that habit, you can move toward a more formal practice of conducting a one-question pre-assessment at the beginning of every lesson and analyzing the data with your students. We will also explore this technique in greater detail in the next section. The key is to start small, solidify good habits, and challenge yourself to move beyond the artificial limits of your comfort zone.

EXAMPLES OF FEEDBACK FROM PEERS

Formative Assessment: Formative assessment is assessment for learning, not of learning; it is meant to inform instruction and not evaluate a student's final level of performance. There are hundreds of ways to engage in formative assessment. To truly capitalize on formative assessment as feedback from students, we need to look at the results to measure our instruction, not student performance. We use formative assessment to informally evaluate our instruction, and we are more likely to make the necessary adjustments to maximize student learning.

One Question Right-Off-the-Bat Strategy: This is a great strategy that blends the benefits of pre-assessment with formative assessment. The strategy is quite simple in design but challenging to incorporate consistently. You start the class period with a one-question formative assessment about what you are *about* to teach. Then, create a multiple-choice question with incorrect answers, or distractors, carefully crafted to illuminate common misunderstandings. If you have access to electronic devices such as Chromebooks, clickers, or tablets, have students respond using these tools. Display the results in a simple bar graph or pie chart and discuss the results so the students understand what their responses say about their understanding. Finally, refine your lesson for that day based on the results. This is a transformative practice that has been demonstrated to significantly increase student performance.

Focus Group: Using focus groups serves as a fantastic, though underused, way to gather feedback directly from students. Focus groups work best when the feedback you are seeking from your students is complex and can be considered from multiple perspectives. To establish a focus group, you first need to identify the concept being explored. For example, you may want to know more about how your chemistry labs reinforce the critical concepts that show up on summative assessments.

The first step is to write three to five simple open-ended questions that will spark a conversation among your students. You then assemble a group of four to six students and establish a time to interview them using established questions. During the interview, it is your job to facilitate the conversation and take good notes. You want your students to feel comfortable sharing their responses and engaging with one another during the focus group session. The next step is to conduct a theme analysis looking for the big ideas that emerged from the focus group.

Next, you should share these themes with the entire class letting them know how the focus group helped you gain this new understanding. Finally, institute some changes based on your newfound insight.

Survey Your Students: When you survey your students, you demonstrate that their opinions matter. By surveying, you can quickly and efficiently collect a significant amount of feedback. When developing surveys, make sure your students have the information and skill set to respond in a meaningful way. This may take practice for both you and your students. Writing surveys can be complex, so keep it simple. Ten or fewer questions should do the trick. It is imperative you share the results with your students to demonstrate that you value their feedback. Using electronic platforms, such as Google forms, allows you to quickly generate a visual representation of their data for you to share and discuss with your students.

Fist-to-Five: The ubiquitous fist-to-five strategy serves as a way to engage your students in the process of providing feedback quickly. The first step is to make a statement to your students with which your students can either agree or disagree. For instance, you might want to know how clearly your group of seventh-grade math students understands how to apply the Pythagorean theorem to the geometry problem you are all exploring.

You would say, "OK, fist-to-five on this statement: I understand how to use the Pythagorean theorem to solve this problem." Now it is your students' turn to respond with a fist-to-five. Students should raise their hand with their corresponding number of fingers displayed—a fist demonstrating a strong disagreement with this statement and a five being a strong agreement. This strategy requires a high degree of trust within your classroom community as you are asking students to potentially publicly share misconceptions. Practicing with small, nonthreatening statements builds the trust to leverage this fantastic strategy fully. To simplify this strategy for younger learners, you could use the same strategy with a three-point scale of thumbs up, down, or sideways.

The key to harnessing the self-efficacy building potential of this strategy is to look at the data you collect truly as feedback. Remember that feedback should inspire reflection. Therefore, you must consider the feedback you received from your students, even if it's in the simple form of a fist or five fingers and reflect on the information you glean. It is not enough to ask the question and simply receive a response. If you keep this in mind, these simple strategies can go a long way to bolstering your self-efficacy and sending a clear message to your students about the importance of their voice.

Co-constructing Instructional Rubrics: If you are on board for an advanced strategy to collect feedback from your students, consider co-constructing a rubric about instructional practices. Many teachers and students co-construct rubrics about student work products. Turning that strategy on its head, we can communicate to our students that we are partners in the learning process.

With this strategy, you must consider the developmental level of your students. Although this strategy tends to be used more readily with high school students, you certainly could adapt it for younger learners. The first step in this process is to engage in a conversation with your students regarding the type of instruction that works best for them. Once you agree upon a few factors the class feels work well and you know to be best practice, create a simple three-point rubric with "3" being the highest level.

Once you have completed the rubric, your students will consult the rubric, rate the performance, and provide feedback. Although this may feel emotionally risky, consider that the same process happens every day with the roles reversed. Not only will this sort of strategy provide you with meaningful feedback from your students and, thus, positively impact your self-efficacy, but it will also increase your students' likelihood of accepting your feedback on their learning performance.

THE FEEDBACK DEVELOPMENT PROCESS

Take a moment to reflect on the Focus and Influence Model of self-efficacy development. You have learned that this model explains that thriving teachers follow a predictable career path through the five contributing factors of teacher self-efficacy. How do the concepts of refined focus on students and expanding influence describe the three stages of seeking and valuing feedback: feedback from authority figures, feedback from peers, and feedback from students?

Although the career path with this factor is predicated on refined focus on students, there is still ample opportunity to broaden your self-efficacy horizons through expanded influence. Refer back to your results on the Thriving Teacher Inventory. How would you describe your skill set related to effectively receiving feedback from authority figures? How frequently do you engage in the practice of giving and receiving meaningful feedback from peers? How can you improve your ability to engage your students in the craft of providing you authentic feedback? Do the results of the Thrive Inventory match your intuition? Remember to use the results of the Thrive Inventory to help you focus your reading on the portions that are most important to you and your career self-efficacy journey.

CHARTING YOUR FEEDBACK PATHWAY

How can you take what you have learned and develop some actionable goals to refine your self-reflective skills? Based on what you have read and your results from the Thrive Inventory, how would you describe your skills in authentically seeking and valuing feedback?

As you consider the progression from one stage to the next on the feedback continuum, keep in mind the Focus and Influence Model you read about in chapter 6. This model explains that the path from one stage to the next in any of the Five Thrive Factors is fueled by a refined focus on students or expanding influence. Do you think refining your focus on students or expanding your influence on other professionals would prove more beneficial to your feedback skill set development? If you do not mind writing in your book, jot down your Thrive Inventory score next to each feedback stage.

MAXIMIZING FEEDBACK FROM AUTHORITY FIGURES

Novice teachers are presented with a paradoxical contradiction in the way they relate to feedback from authority figures. Novice teachers depend on feedback from authority figures to build their burgeoning self-efficacy. Leaders must provide new teachers the feedback to let them know they are on the right course or point out any necessary course adjustments. At the same time, many teachers are hesitant to seek out this sort of feedback out of insecurities. The most important act teachers at this stage can take is to learn how to accept feedback and then wholeheartedly seek it out.

It is important to remember that skillfully receiving feedback from authority figures is not just crucial for new teachers. All educators can continue to support their self-efficacy by maximizing the impact feedback from their boss has on their practice. The added benefit of improving your ability to effectively receive feedback from authority figures is that it can naturally lead to opportunities to receive feedback from peers.

Accepting and valuing feedback is a skill that is best developed by creating habits. Teachers at this stage in their development must find opportunities to receive feedback. The first foray into proactively seeking out feedback from authority figures should be in a low-risk environment. Asking an instructional coach or a mentor to observe a lesson and provide feedback is a great place to start. You could also be more direct and let the coach or mentor know that you are working on developing the skills to effectively receive feedback. Instructional coaches are among the most highly trained professionals when it comes to the art of giving and receiving feedback.

Preparation also increases the likelihood that you will effectively receive feedback. If a principal has recently observed you and scheduled a post-observation conference, prepare for that conference. The sort of preparation suggested here may differ from what you traditionally would consider at such a juncture. For example, instead of focusing on answering questions, make sure you also prepare to ask questions. You certainly can plan on being asked a question about what went well and what you could improve next time. Again, there's nothing wrong with these questions, but they just scratch the surface of the latent potential of meaningful feedback.

Consider being transparent with your principal and letting them know something concrete you would like to improve in your practice. Then ask specific questions about this area for potential improvement. It could be something as discrete as providing adequate wait time or something as complex as building a classroom community valuing risk-taking. Better yet, prepare for the feedback by suggesting this area of focus before the observation.

This will not only increase the specificity of the feedback you receive, it will set your principal up to be as successful as possible. It may look easy to come into a classroom with a laptop, sit at a table in the back, and take notes. However, knowing where to focus is a skill in and of itself. Most principals would consider it a gift if you provided them with a potential area of focus.

At the risk of sounding like a broken record, avoid overlooking the need to reflect on the feedback. While you are receiving the feedback, it may be challenging to know what questions to ask. If you are unclear on what the feedback means, make sure you ask, but do not worry if you are simply uncertain how to respond. Give it some time, reflect, and consider how you can leverage the provided feedback to improve your practice.

Resist the urge to be defensive. Defensiveness encourages feedback to be taken out of context. There is no way an outside observer could drop in a classroom and understand all of the layers of context and nuance contributing to that one moment in time. So do not waste your time trying to explain all of the context as it may come across as defensive and an attempt to excuse away the value of the feedback.

If you disagree on a matter of opinion, remember it is just that, an opinion. If there is factual content that is misrepresented, certainly set the record straight, but do so to clarify and authentically receive the feedback. If you receive feedback that confuses you and does not provide a clear next step, ask for clarification. You might say something like, "So what I'm hearing you say is that you would like me to consider differentiating my instruction by incorporating more small group work." Remember that feedback is a dialogue, not a monologue. It should flow in both directions.

MOVING TOWARD FEEDBACK FROM PEERS

Sometimes we set goals because we have to and sometimes we set them because we want to. "Want-to" goals hold great power. "Want-to" goals are not mandated and align with our convictions and beliefs. They fuel resiliency and self-efficacy. Typically, teachers who seek feedback from peers do so because they want to, not because an authority figure demands it. Teachers who value feedback from peers must commit and actively seek it out. As you read this section, picture the peers you could rely on to share the gift of feedback in your mind's eye.

This proactive approach to seeking and valuing feedback from peers is a powerful aid as teachers progress through their careers. The first step in capitalizing on the power of peer feedback is to make a plan. In this plan, you must consider the type of feedback you find most compelling, the aspect of your teaching for which you desire feedback, and the specific person in your circle of trust from whom you would prefer feedback.

One of the underutilized opportunities to give and receive feedback from peers are your regular meetings with your professional learning community team. If you are fortunate enough to work with a professional learning community team who shares trust and a commitment to the success of one another, you can incorporate a few minor adjustments to reap the benefit of feedback from peers.

A typical element of any PLC meeting is discussing student learning results and the corresponding teaching behaviors that contribute to those results. Typically, at this point, the conversation shifts to practices that should be continued and which should be reconsidered. By pausing before deciding on the next steps, the team could capitalize on the opportunity to provide feedback specifically about the teaching practices discussed. This will not only establish the habit of proactively seeking feedback but it will also likely result in a deeper understanding of the teaching practices that resulted in the student learning at the center of the conversation.

A PLC team could also incorporate direct observation of team members with scheduled subsequent meetings dedicated to giving and receiving feedback. This sort of professional learning opportunity serves as the perfect venue for practicing the art of giving and receiving feedback in a safe space. Take a moment to consider the team with whom you regularly work as a PLC. Would you feel emotionally safe receiving feedback from any member of that team? Would you feel comfortable offering feedback to any member of the team? If the answer is yes to both of those questions, you and your team are ready to support your collective efficacy through the power of peer-to-peer feedback.

LEVERAGING FEEDBACK FROM STUDENTS

Who better to provide you feedback about your teaching than those you teach? Your students have observed more of your teaching than anyone else. They are the experts.

But remember, you are still the teacher, and you need to teach your students how to provide quality feedback every bit as much as you need to increase your capacity for receiving feedback.

If you are ready to build your repertoire of skills to receive feedback from students effectively, consider the following five-step plan. The first step is to harness student agency as you develop your students' understanding of the value of their feedback. Next, you should work with your students to build the basic skills in offering feedback. Once they understand the fundamentals of good feedback, you can create space and time for them to formulate and offer feedback. It is then time to fill their toolbox with specific skills and strategies to give feedback. Finally, it is your turn to demonstrate change based on their feedback.

Harness Student Agency: Students with a high sense of agency believe they have significant influence and control over their learning. The concept of personalized learning is philosophically predicated on the power of student agency. If students believe they have the authority to offer feedback to their teacher, their agency skyrockets! Be direct and straightforward as you set out to harness student agency. For example, the conversation could look something like this:

> *You*: I have realized I could do a better job if I knew how you felt about my teaching. I set a goal to get feedback from all of you so I can become a better teacher.
>
> *Student 1*: How are *we* supposed to give *you* feedback! Isn't that your job?
>
> *You:* Well, part of my job is to give you feedback about your learning, but I believe it should go both ways. Everything I do here is so you can learn. It only makes sense that I should hear directly from all of you.
>
> *Student 2*: I have NO idea how I could ever give you feedback. You're a good teacher, and we all like you.
>
> *You:* Well, I appreciate that, but we can all improve, and I really want to be the best I can be, and I want your help! As far as knowing what to do, don't worry. We will spend a few minutes every day for the next two weeks learning what it means to give good feedback.

This sort of conversation sets the stage for you and your students to view this goal as a partnership. Once you embark on the next steps, continue to support student agency by letting them know how important their input is in the learning process. Once your students begin to believe in their impact and develop a sense of agency, everything else in this process falls into place much more easily.

Build Their Skills: Back in chapter 3, you learned the three characteristics of effective feedback. Effective feedback is thought-provoking, specific, and reciprocal. Furthermore, feedback can come in three forms including encouraging, critical, and data based. A quick review is important as these three characteristics and three feedback styles will create the basis for the skills your students will develop.

Create Space and Time: Students need space and time to hone their craft. As an educator, you know it can be challenging to offer great feedback, and we all went to college for it! Make sure you provide your students the opportunity to practice formulating their feedback before they offer the feedback. It certainly can be anxiety-inducing to receive feedback, but it can be even worse for a student who has to offer feedback about their teacher. Start with low-risk feedback opportunities in groups or pairs to keep emotions in check.

Teach Specific Skills: It is time to teach your students specific strategies such as fist-to-five or exit slips. Each time you introduce a new strategy, offer time to practice. Eventually, your students will begin naturally offering feedback when it works for them.

Demonstrate Change: If you want your students to continue providing feedback and improving their skills, demonstrate you are listening by adjusting your practices. If a student offers feedback and you make adjustments, announce it. It could sound like this: "Ahmir let me know he wanted me to provide more strong examples of your Great Depression Perspectives project. Here are three exemplars from last year. Let's talk about what makes them work. Thanks for the suggestion, Ahmir!" When your students know their feedback matters, their sense of agency will blossom, improving the feedback.

COACHES CORNER

In the previous Coaches Corner, we explored the way coaches prioritize self-reflection with teachers whom they coach. These same coaches rely heavily on feedback as the mechanism to encourage that self-reflection. Feedback is the heart of excellent instructional coaching. This is true if you are a formal instructional coach or if you rely on coaching in your job as a principal or other instructional leader. How can you use this skill set to support teachers in their ability to utilize feedback?

If you coach teachers, you are uniquely positioned to help teachers progress through the feedback career stages. When looking for opportunities to increase teachers' feedback capacity, consider the *Law & Order* rule of professional learning.[1] In every episode of *Law & Order* or any other crime investigation show, the detectives look for motive, means, and opportunity. When they find all three of these elements for a suspect, they have caught their criminal. When you find all three of these elements for the teacher you are working with, you have struck professional learning gold.

Motive is all about the "why." For the detective, it is determining why a suspect might have been motivated to commit the crime. As a coach, it is about helping the teacher develop a motive for why they want to progress through the feedback career stages. Remember, "motive" is the root word of "motivate"!

You must start with motive. If teachers do not understand the why behind the need to improve their skills related to improving their practice based on feedback, they will not move forward. Your first step is to help the teacher understand the self-efficacy boosting power of feedback. You could use tools such as the Thrive Inventory to develop a clear understanding of their current placement on the feedback continuum.

The motive can look very different depending on their placement on that continuum. For example, if you are working with a novice teacher who is just beginning to develop the skill set necessary to receive feedback from an authority figure, the "why" would be very pragmatic. You could look at their relationship with their supervisor and the benefits of demonstrating willingness to respond to their supervisor's feedback.

If the teacher you are working with is on the opposite end of the feedback development continuum and is ready to transform student learning, your coaching support would look very different. You could start by encouraging them to reflect on a simple question: how do you know your students fully benefit from your style of instruction? Then, you could unearth opportunity galore by using a strategy such as the "five whys" previously discussed. You could also engage in student-centered coaching by focusing on one student who might not appear fully engaged. Finally, you could illuminate a strong motive by coaching your colleague to reflect on the benefit of seeking feedback from the seemingly disengaged student.

When detectives consider "means," they assess whether or not the suspect has the skills and tools necessary to commit the crime. When you consider "means" from a coaching perspective, you assess the skills and tools required to achieve success at the various stages in the feedback career progression. Tools could include tangible items such as protocols, surveys, or assessment tools. Skills could come in the form of aptitudes, predispositions, or strategies.

We refer to this factor as "seeking and valuing" feedback for a particular reason. The "seeking" of feedback pertains directly to the requisite strategies and skills. This factor's "valuing" portion refers to the dispositions and mindset necessary to deftly progress through the feedback career stages. For example, suppose you hit a roadblock with the teacher you are coaching to increase their feedback capacity. In that case, you must first discern if the area for improvement is concentrated on the equation's seeking or valuing side.

If you find the teacher you are working with would benefit from skill development in strategies and techniques to seek feedback, you can employ the strategies we've discussed so far in this chapter. If you determine the area of concern is more closely related to the predispositions and mindset necessary to progress to the new stage, you likely should spend more time reinforcing their skill set at their current stage while gently coaching them to a broader understanding of the benefits at the next stage.

Opportunity is all about timing. When detectives consider the opportunity for a suspect to have committed a crime, they must consider time and location. When you delve into the world of opportunity as a coach, you also consider time and location. Teachers must have an opportunity to practice the skills necessary to leverage feedback in their classroom with their students. As a coach, you have ample potential to influence these opportunities.

As a coach, the best way for you to increase opportunity for your colleagues is to provide an occasion to engage in authentic practice gathering and responding to feedback. Depending on your colleague's career stage, this practice could be related to gathering feedback from authority figures, peers, or students. You should always focus on increasing teachers' capacity to succeed with a more diverse group of students. You can do this by observing the teacher in action, providing feedback, and encouraging self-reflection.

CHAPTER REFLECTIONS

1. How would you describe your feedback habits?
2. How has your ability to meaningfully respond to feedback evolved throughout your career?
3. Reflect on a time in your career when you received painful feedback? What made it painful? Was there anything you could have done differently to make it less painful?
4. What was the best feedback you have ever received? Who provided the feedback, and what made it so good?
5. How can you increase your opportunity to receive feedback that helps you thrive?

ACTION PLAN

In the last chapter, you reflected on who you want to become as an educator. Take out your reflection and read it back to yourself. Now it is time for you to consider the feedback you need to realize that vision. Consider where you are on the feedback career stage continuum based on the results of the Thrive Inventory and your intuition. Where do you want to go, and who can help you get there?

How can you leverage feedback from authority figures, peers, and your students to help you progress? Who are the authority figures and peers who will provide you with the most honest and inspiring feedback?

Consider the feedback factor. How can you capitalize on feedback to thrive and to move toward your vision for you? Maybe it is establishing a peer group to share feedback. Perhaps you want to work more regularly with an instructional coach. Maybe you are ready to get wild and find ways to maximize your impact by seeking feedback directly from your students. It is your journey. It is time for you to pledge one thing you will do to move toward that goal. Make it small. Make it manageable. Make it happen!

9

Collaboration Career Stages

While some people enjoy traveling alone, most people enhance their journey by traveling with friends and family. Traveling with others encourages you to try new things you may not have experienced if you were alone. Traveling with company allows you to enjoy the events at a deeper stage by sharing emotional experiences. Traveling with others, at its core, builds relationships. This same dynamic exists with professional collaboration and self-efficacy development.

Collaboration with colleagues is a natural contributing factor to a teacher's self-efficacy. Andrew Carnegie said, "Teamwork . . . is the ability to direct individual accomplishments toward organizational objectives. It is the fuel that allows common people to attain uncommon results."

How do teachers collaboratively feed their self-efficacy and collective efficacy as they navigate their career paths? Well, it depends. It depends on which domain of teacher self-efficacy they are aiming to improve. Thriving teachers access collaboration as a way to support all four domains of teacher self-efficacy: instruction, classroom community, student engagement, and self-care.

It depends on their stage of experience. A thriving teacher can progress through three career stages of collaboration. In the earliest stages of a career, teachers seek mentors as a means of supporting their self-efficacy. In the mid-career stages, they engage in professional networks to expand their influence and their perspectives. Finally, at the most advanced stages, teachers feed their self-efficacy by coaching peers.

Finally, it depends on who they are as individuals. A vast array of factors influence a teacher's personal and professional identity. Professional identity is a specific form of social identity. There are three levels of a teacher's social or professional identity including:

- *Core:* Characteristics that make us unique individuals. For instance, I value diversity and equity.
- *Chosen:* Characteristics we decide to use to describe who we are. For instance, I am a teacher.
- *Given:* Attributes or conditions that we have no control over. For instance, I am a fifty-year-old white woman.[1]

These three levels of professional identity answer the question, who am I as a teacher?

Teachers' professional identities directly influence how they will collaborate throughout their careers to support their individual and collective efficacy. If a colleague asked you who you are as a teacher, how would you answer? How would the answer to that question impact how you collaborate with others?

As you look at the characteristics of the three levels of collaboration, consider the answer to the questions above. Remember, thriving teachers naturally progress through these stages. However, the rate at which teachers progress varies greatly. Some thriving teachers may quickly move to stage 2 or 3. For others, it may be a thirty-year journey. By understanding each stage, and how you can move from one stage to the next, you can maximize your efforts to boost and maintain your teacher self-efficacy.

CHARACTERISTICS OF COLLABORATION

Seeking Mentoring	Engaging in Professional Networks	Coaching Peers
Focused on Teaching	Focused on Learning	Focused on Leading
Influenced by Others	Learning to Influence	Influencing Others
Defined Perspectives	Diverse Perspectives	Expanding Perspectives
Internally Structured	Externally Structured	Flexible

Look back to your Thriving Teacher Inventory results to help you explore your use of collaboration. First, complete the table below with results from the collaboration portion of the inventory. Once again, you can use the results to leverage collaboration for your self-efficacy.

Collaboration			
Stage 1: Seeking Mentoring	Stage 2: Engaging in Professional Networks	Stage 3: Coaching Peers	Total Collaboration Score

Consider the following scale as you reflect on your total score:

25–30: High collaborative efficacy
19–24: Moderate collaborative efficacy
13–18: Emerging collaborative efficacy
 <13: Low collaborative efficacy

The highest possible score for each stage is ten. A score of six or below indicates that capitalizing on mentorship could be an appropriate next step. A score of seven or higher indicates a belief in your ability to capitalize on mentorship. Use these results as you did in the previous sections to guide you on your learning to personalize your journey.

STAGE 1: SEEKING MENTORING

When you think of those who have mentored you, do you think of current circumstances or your earlier teaching experiences? Many teachers' experiences with mentors peak when they are first hired and quickly fade to nonexistent. This is not to suggest more experienced teachers do not benefit from professional mentors. Research suggests that teachers in the earliest stages of their career rely more exclusively on mentors to fuel their self-efficacy.

Most school districts typically assign mentors to new teachers for a period between one and three years. These mentorship programs are typically designed to acclimate the new teacher to the school and to build their basic instructional skills. Mentorship programs have garnered increased attention as teacher burnout has become a topic of national concern.

We have already learned that high levels of teacher self-efficacy, specifically coupled with efficacy related to self-care, can significantly reduce the risk of teacher burnout. How could districts structure mentorship programs to maximize their impact on teacher self-efficacy? The answer lies in focus. Mentorship programs that are heavily focused on procedural compliance may limit self-efficacy by stifling a new teacher's creativity.

Developing mentorship programs that balance training and inspiration is the key to unleashing a new teacher's self-efficacy. Studies demonstrate preservice teachers have higher levels of self-efficacy than teachers in the first three years of their careers. Experts attribute this phenomenon to the heavy dose of reality new teachers face when they emerge from the insulated safety of their preservice programs. High-quality mentorship programs can bridge that gap.

Mentors should be trained in the art and science of inspiring teachers to believe in themselves. This starts by ensuring only inspirational teachers with high levels of self-efficacy serve as mentors. This should be followed by heavy doses of encouraging feedback and structures to foster self-reflection. Imagine every new teacher being matched with a thriving mentor who has the training and mindset to tap into the beautiful idealism held by most preservice teachers.

Mentoring is a critical structure to combat our growing teacher shortage crisis. Low teacher self-efficacy is a recipe for burnout. The data on early teacher burnout is horrifying.

- More than one in five (22%) teachers in 2011 were under the age of 30, and the proportion of teachers 50 and older dropped from 42 percent in 2005 to 31 percent in 2011.[2]
- 17% of teachers leave the profession in the first five years.[3]
- During the COVID 19 pandemic, over 50% of teachers stated it is very likely or somewhat likely they will leave the teaching profession in the next two years.[4]
- Until the Great Recession of 2008, the supply and demand of teachers was consistent. Then, when districts recovered financially, they found it more challenging to hire teachers. Then COVID hit. According to the Economic Policy Institute in their 2019 report on teacher shortages, by 2025, the projected supply of teachers will fall nearly 200,000 teachers short of the demand.[5]

What does this data tell us? We need to do a better job of recruiting teachers to the profession. Furthermore, when we hire them, we better do our very best to support them. Mentoring is one of the best ways to support new teachers. It is a collaborative structure that can be personalized to meet teachers where they are in their learning journey. Mentoring builds strong, confident, and efficacious teachers.

CHARACTERISTICS OF MENTORSHIP

Focused on Teaching: Mentors typically focus their collaborative support on teacher actions. These include topics such as lesson planning, classroom management, basic instructional strategies, and the like. Essentially, they cover Teaching 101. This makes intuitive sense as they are typically working with novice teachers who require essential support. Mentoring bridges the gap between preservice teaching and the exciting world of first jobs! New teachers require this essential support to boost their self-efficacy, as the realities of the job begin to threaten to erode exuberant preservice optimism.

Influenced by Others: The collaborative support teachers receive through mentoring is heavily influenced by others. The others include the mentor themselves, principals, and district administrators who designed the mentor program curriculum. This certainly makes sense, as most teachers who receive mentoring have little to no experience. Their self-efficacy is boosted as they learn more about operationalizing the skills and strategies they learned in their preservice programs.

There is, however, an inherent risk to this typical structure. Mentors begin working with teachers when their self-efficacy is at an all-time (albeit inflated) high. If their voice is not included in the collaborative support process, the self-efficacy boosting power of mentorship can wane and begin to have a detrimental impact. We ought not squelch the enthusiasm of new teachers. Instead, we must embrace it and find ways to include their fresh perspectives to drive the mentor-mentee collaborative relationship. In this way, both the mentee and mentor can enjoy the self-efficacy boosting power of their collaboration.

Defined Perspectives: Collaboration presents opportunities to learn with others and broaden perspectives. By seeking mentors as a means of improving self-efficacy, the perspectives are defined and predetermined. Mentorship is a collegial relationship between just two people. Teachers who rely on a mentor as their primary collaborative support are limited to the mentor's perspective. This is neither good nor bad. It is just limited.

Internally Structured: Mentorship is a structure defined by the district or school in which it is implemented. These programs tend to be relatively rigid as they meet any combination of statutory, policy-based, or licensing agency mandates. This internal structure allows for minimal guarantees of content and topics, but it also places an artificial cap on potential.

STAGE 2: ENGAGING IN PROFESSIONAL NETWORKS

Professional networks have emerged as a more viable collaborative structure for teachers in recent years. Professional networks are groups of teachers who share professional interests. Teachers join professional networks to voluntarily collaborate with and learn from others. The recent proliferation of online tools for teachers has expanded professional network opportunities as they do not require travel, registration fees, or administrative permission.

Some professional networks include local, state, or national organizations such as ASCD (Association for Supervision and Curriculum Development), the National Council of Teachers of Mathematics, or the Association for Middle Level Education (AMLE). They also include online communities like #kinderchat or #Edchat on Twitter or Facebook Groups for School on Edshelf. Finally, they include informal local groups who conduct book talks, focused discussions, or debates.

Research suggests teachers with more than five years of experience are more likely to join professional networks to support their self-efficacy. However, teachers in their first few years may lack the confidence to contribute to professional networks. They may also not have the time to volunteer hours outside of the workday for these endeavors.

Teachers support their self-efficacy through participating in these sorts of networks in two ways. First, they learn from others. It is always easier for teachers to incorporate new ideas into practice when they seek out the new skills of their own accord. Second, they support their self-efficacy by expanding their influence and sharing ideas with a broader audience.

CHARACTERISTICS OF PROFESSIONAL NETWORKS

Focused on Learning: Unlike mentoring, teachers engaging in professional networks have opportunities to focus on student learning and teaching practices. Mentors necessarily focus on teaching fundamentals, while professional networks can freely focus their energies on any direction they see fit. Teachers who engage in professional networks can balance the focus between sides of the teaching and learning continuum.

A plethora of formal and informal professional networks have emerged in the past few years dedicated to social and emotional learning. The founders of these organizations dedicated the time to develop these networks out of a perceived student need. @SELearningEDU, a Twitter-based network dedicated to "sharing strategies and resources on social-emotional learning for parents, educators, & mental health professionals," for example, posts vibrant, student-focused discussions.[6] With nearly 50,000 subscribers, this organization has become one node in a vast web of resources and networks allowing teachers to collaborate and support their self-efficacy by expanding their influence.

Learning to Influence: Teachers who engage in professional networks gain opportunities to practice leadership and influencing skills. Teachers interested in expanding their influence and honing their leadership skills can find it challenging to break into established social networks in their schools. By collaborating with colleagues throughout their state or the nation, they can embrace opportunities to influence in a less-threatening environment.

Teachers who participate in professional networks also enhance their influencing skills by learning from others in the network. Jeremy is an elementary teacher who has worked in the same school in an exceedingly small rural district for the past nine years. His grade-level teammates are all very experienced and tend to dismiss his ideas. This dismissiveness began to erode his self-efficacy, so he decided to do something about it.

Jeremy joined a few Twitter chats. He found #CultureEd amazingly supportive of his self-efficacy. Countless other teachers were advocating for changes to education to improve school and classroom culture. This was the student-centered topic he struggled to inspire his teammates to embrace. He was a passive participant in the chat for about two months before he plucked up the courage to post. He said the first time he had a tweet retweeted, his self-efficacy skyrocketed. He credits his participation in this chat as inspiration for his growing advocacy back in his school with his team. The trick is to find a professional network that speaks to who you are as a teacher. There are countless opportunities out there. If you cannot find one that matches a specific area of interest, perhaps you can start your own.

Diverse Perspectives: Professional networks function as ideal settings to learn from colleagues with diverse perspectives. When Jeremy joined Twitter chats, he sought out topics of interest to him. Even though he personalized his selection based on his own identity and interests, he found the diversity of experience and perspective among other participants refreshing. Jeremey grew up less than twenty miles from the school where he now teaches. He went to college less than an hour away. These Twitter chats expanded his horizons and exposed him to a whole new world of ideas and perspectives he found quite invigorating.

Externally Structured: Professional networks are typically structured externally. This means people established the structure of the group outside of their district or school. This allows teachers to seek out the specific professional networks that interest them. This applies to the subject matter of the network and the style of collaboration. For example, a teacher may be interested in learning how to leverage technology to increase student engagement, and they may want to engage asynchronously. There is a professional network for that. The personalization that these externally structured networks allows for enables teachers to pursue very specific avenues to positively impact their self-efficacy.

STAGE 3: PEER COACHING

Both mentoring and coaching are two-way social endeavors. Coaching blends the transformative power of feedback with the power of collaboration. Feedback provides input but coaching changes habits. When teachers shift their collaborative focus to peer coaching, they no longer are solely on the receiving end of the relationship. As a peer coach, a teacher's perspective shifts to that of a leader. As a leader, the peer coach expands their influence. The peer coach can bolster their self-efficacy as well as the self-efficacy of those with whom they collaborate.

Teachers can seek to serve as a peer coach in a number of ways. They can pursue formal opportunities to coach others by transitioning to an instructional coach position. Instructional coaching has recently risen in popularity and now represents a major slice of the total investment in professional learning. Districts are moving away from the practice of sending teachers to conferences and workshops and moving toward a job-embedded professional learning structure supported directly by instructional coaches.

Informal opportunities for teachers to serve as peer coaches abound. Often, seizing these opportunities is merely a matter of shifting one's perspective. For instance, a teacher may be a member of a PLC team that has worked together for years. By assuming the role of peer coach, a teacher could positively influence other members of the team. Simply asking open-ended questions that start with phrases such as "have you considered . . . ?" or "how did the students respond when you . . . ?" helps teachers support the self-efficacy of their colleagues while bolstering their own self-efficacy through expanding influence.

CHARACTERISTICS OF PEER COACHING

Focused on Leading: A teacher who decides to engage in peer coaching assumes a leadership position that significantly enhances their self-efficacy. Typically, well-experienced teachers gravitate to peer-coaching roles as they seek opportunities to expand their influence and boost their self-efficacy. A peer coach has every opportunity to focus dialogue with colleagues on teaching practices or student learning. Regardless of the focus, a distinguishing characteristic of this style of collaboration is the presence of leadership.

Influencing Others: Peer coaching presents the perfect opportunity to harness the power of expanding influence. As a peer coach, teachers can bring to bear all they have learned as a thriving teacher for an ever-expanding group of students. The opportunity to influence others through peer coaching is a direct application of expanding influence to support self-efficacy. Peer coaches reflect on what is important to them and coach others to understand and apply the related principles.

Expanding Perspectives: Anyone who has engaged in any level of peer coaching knows there is no better way to learn something than to teach it to someone else. By coaching someone else, you learn a great deal about their perspective. By tapping into the learner's perspective and personalizing the coaching, you are able to coach more effectively. Ideally, both the coach and the coached end up with a broadened perspective.

Brené Brown has described the four steps to showing empathy. They include:

1. Perspective-taking or putting yourself in someone else's shoes;
2. Staying out of judgment and listening;
3. Recognizing emotion in another person that you have maybe felt before; and
4. Communicating that you can recognize that emotion.[7]

The first step of perspective-taking allows a peer coach to deeply understand the emotional and practical concerns of the colleagues with whom they work. By expanding perspective, a coach becomes ever more equipped to help others who may share similar perspectives.

Flexible: Peer coaching can be flexible. A peer coach can decide how often and with whom you engage in coaching. Teachers can pursue formal opportunities to peer coach, such as seeking a job as an instructional coach, or they can simply make themselves available to lesser experienced colleagues.

COLLABORATION AND THE FOUR DOMAINS OF TEACHER SELF-EFFICACY

How does collaboration feed the individual domains of teacher self-efficacy? If you focus your collaboration on instruction, you are most likely to boost your instructional self-efficacy. For example, you could organize a peer network focused on Responsive Classroom structures in an effort to build classroom community. This collaboration would quite likely impact your classroom engagement efficacy. Although collaboration impacts your overall teacher self-efficacy, it is essential to think deeply about improving your efficacy in each domain.

This relationship between the focus of your collaboration and the impact on the most closely related domain makes intuitive sense, but it should also drive your action planning. By examining your results on the Thrive Domain portion of the inventory, you can get a sense of where your relative teacher self-efficacy strengths lie. In each chapter, you can jot down your scores to remind you where you may want to focus your energies. How might collaboration impact your self-efficacy in any or all of the four domains? Think about your connection between self-reflection and the four domains and use that information to guide your professional learning.

MOVING FROM MENTORSHIP TO PROFESSIONAL NETWORKS

If you are a teacher who relies heavily on the mentorship of others to support your self-efficacy, there are opportunities for you to shift your perspective. Of the three styles of collaboration, receiving mentorship is primarily passive. You can much more actively engage as a participant with an equal voice by collaborating as a member of professional networks.

Here is a simple and straightforward five-step process that will allow you to make the shifts necessary to thrive in professional networks. These steps will lead you through the process of initially identifying opportunities for finding your voice. Each step includes a reflective question. Consider your response to each question as you explore this process.

Step 1: Identify your passion and purpose. Clarify the distinction between these two terms when considering your passion and purpose. Passion is the "what" and purpose is the "why." Your passion may be co-teaching. Co-teaching is what drives you. Your purpose may be to create inclusive learning environments for students with disabilities. That is your why. With your why clearly defined, you will refine your search for the appropriate professional network.

Step 2: Explore networks. Searching for the perfect professional network can be an intimidating endeavor. To simplify the process, begin your search where you already feel comfortable. For instance, if you are a prolific Twitter user who follows various thought leaders, search there for your professional network of choice. Perhaps you prefer Facebook. Follow a few of your favorite educational leaders and read their posts looking for mentions of their preferred networks.

Maybe you prefer face-to-face interactions over social media. Most states have some regional collaborative networks designed for teachers. They often offer free or very reasonable professional learning opportunities. Sign up for one of these opportunities and see if you can expand your network with like-minded professionals in neighboring districts. Joining national organizations and subscribing to their journals provides access to enriching professional network opportunities. ASCD, Learning Forward, Teaching Tolerance, and CASEL (Collaborative for Academic, Social, and Emotional Learning) are a few popular and worthwhile organizations to consider.

Step 3: Join and acclimate. All of these organizations and online platforms approach their collaboration opportunities differently. There is no one-size-fits-all solution to finding the right opportunities. If you are exploring free opportunities such as Twitter chats, join one and try it for a few months. It is important not to give up right away as it may take some time for you to acclimate to their norms and means of collaborating. After you try it for a while, do not feel guilty to move on to different opportunities. The effectiveness of the collaboration is measured by your self-efficacy, not by anyone else's opinion.

If you are exploring opportunities to join formal organizations, you can still do so with negligible risk. Many organizations such as Learning Forward and ASCD offer free resources that will give you a sense of what the organization is all about. If one of these organizations piques your interest, talk to your principal to see if it would be appropriate to use your classroom budget to subscribe.

Attending conferences can be costly, but some districts will support this practice if you create a plan to bring your learning back to your colleagues. If you are involved in a timely and innovative practice, take a risk and write a conference breakout session proposal. Many of these national organizations have state affiliates looking for practical presentations from practitioners in the field. Some districts are more likely to allow you to attend a conference if you are presenting. It is always a good idea to ask your principal about this before you take the time to write the proposal. The key is to keep your eyes open and look for opportunities aligned with your learning style and areas of interest.

Step 4: Engage and influence. After you find your collaborative opportunity in a professional network that meets your needs, it is time to engage. For many teachers, actively engaging in the network can be more challenging than initially joining. This is especially true for introverted teachers. Start small with a tweet, Facebook post, or share something you learned from a formal organization.

Combining the power of social media with the content of a national organization is also a fantastic way to dip your toes in the water of engaging in professional networks. Most professional networks maintain a dynamic social media presence. Follow one of these organizations and retweet something of interest. Getting your first like or retweet is a terrific way to boost your self-efficacy.

Step 5: Act. Step 5 answers the question, "So what?" After you have engaged in a professional network for a while, look for opportunities to bring back your new learning to your practice. Once you start implementing the student-focused practices you learned through engaging in a professional network, you build your repertoire of content to discuss and share. This cyclical process of engaging, acting, and sharing can generate perpetual energy to fuel your self-efficacy.

Better yet, take back something you have learned through your engagement in a professional network and share it in your school with one of your collaborative groups. For instance, a teacher could learn about Universal Design for Learning (UDL) by engaging in a CASEL online seminar.[8] This teacher could then share their inspiration with a PLC team and encourage them to participate in a book study about UDL. As you can see in this example, collaboration can transform typical linear growth into exponential growth by simply bringing more voices to the table.

ADVANCING FROM PROFESSIONAL NETWORKS TO PEER COACH

Let us pick up right where we left off. Do you remember the teacher who learned about UDL and then brought ideas back to her PLC? By assuming a leadership role with her PLC and expanding her influence, she has moved into the realm of peer coaching. If you are looking for an opportunity to expand your influence by serving as a peer coach, consider the following three steps.

Step 1: Find a natural connection. First, you must find natural connections between you and your colleagues. It is critical your peer coaching is invited. If you are attempting to offer peer coaching to someone who is not in a position to accept it, your self-efficacy could be eroded. This erosion of self-efficacy could damage the relationship. Do you work with a colleague with less experience who often seeks you out for an opinion? Do you work on a curricular team with members who rely on you to take the lead? Does your principal often come to you before rolling out a new initiative? The answers to each of these questions can guide you to a natural connection you could leverage by coaching.

Step 2: Listen. High-quality coaching involves much more listening than speaking—the most effective coaching results in self-discovery. Expert coaches know how to ask the right questions that illuminate the hidden understandings all teachers possess. Great coaches do not, and should not, have all the answers. This is why finding natural connections is so important. If there is no strong relationship between the coach and the coached, dialogue is stilted and conversations tend to lean too heavily on coach talk. There are enough people telling teachers what to do. We do not need to add to that list.

Step 3: Support. Finally, and most importantly, a coach must support the goals and aspirations of the teachers with whom they work. By leveraging natural connections and listening attentively, a coach can help teachers clarify their goals. Coaches have the opportunity to support teachers as they work to accomplish their goals. Coaches can serve as accountability partners who periodically check in with partner teachers regarding progress toward their goals.

A coach may play a more direct role in supporting a teacher's goals. Coaches can capitalize on their unique perspective as observers and partners to unearth high-impact coaching opportunities. Barriers preventing teachers from meeting their goals are often hidden in the unconscious or subconscious habits the teacher cannot see for themselves. A coach who follows these three steps will serve as the trusted collaborative colleague who can help elucidate these barriers and coach for success.

COACHES CORNER

A coach can play a vital role in support of teacher collaboration. A coach can link teachers together into meaningful networks. If you are a coach seeking opportunities to facilitate effective collaboration, consider these three potential opportunities to capitalize on similarities: similar goals, similar interests, or similar responsibilities.

Similar Goals: As a coach, you are privy to many of the teachers' goals. These can be required goals as part of the evaluation process or individual goals set by the teacher. Some groups of teachers develop shared goals. By comparing the goals of the teacher with whom you work, you can identify opportunities for collaboration.

For example, you may find that high school teachers who teach elective courses have goals related to student goal setting. You could connect these teachers and facilitate collaborative learning. You can offer your support by facilitating the dialogue or covering for a classroom teacher to allow for common prep time.

You can ensure a meaningful experience by linking the coaching to results. Consider how these will be measured and track progress toward that goal. This is a direct path to boosted self-efficacy.

Similar Interests: If you have the opportunity to facilitate collaboration among teachers who share similar interests, you also have the opportunity to facilitate transformation. As we have learned, seeking feedback and collaborating support self-efficacy. Collaborating around a shared interest maximizes the potential impact of coaching as it directly connects with teachers' passion and purpose.

For example, you could have the opportunity to work with a group of middle school teachers who are intrigued by the concept of personalized learning. As a coach, you could help foster their collaboration by curating resources, including videos, organization contacts, and books. To dig a little deeper, you could find a rubric or inventory to help the teachers gain insight into their understanding of the concept. Deeper still, you could engage in some shared reading followed up by co-constructing a rubric. Finally, you could use the rubric to facilitate some fantastic coaching!

Similar Responsibilities: Coaches often collaboratively group teachers by similar responsibilities. This sort of grouping has both great potential and significant challenges. The potential rests on the fact that these similar responsibilities naturally occur in a school (i.e., PLCs, content teams, grade level teams). These groups present a very streamlined way to group teachers and access them via their existing meeting structures. In these instances, you can focus your coaching efforts on building a true sense of team with a sense of collective responsibility for the success of all students.

When seeking opportunities to coach for collaboration with teachers who share similar responsibilities, try to streamline their work. Nothing breaks down barriers and opens doors for coaching better than establishing win-win situations where student learning improves and teacher workflow is streamlined. If their collaborative efforts can help them more effectively and efficiently address existing responsibilities, you are much more likely to engage the teachers.

Cara, for instance, is a high school instructional coach who works primarily with English and social studies teachers. While working with individual PLC teams, Cara noticed significant overlap among the interim assessments for each team. She spoke individually with each team. She proposed collaborative coaching around streamlining their assessment process. Coaching led to a transformation resulting in improved student learning outcomes and student engagement.

Cara first facilitated a process for each team clarifying their priority standards. She then stripped away assessment questions that were not aligned to these priorities. Next, they co-created an assessment map where each team listed their priority standards and the corresponding assessment. The teams used this document with Cara's support to develop a process of alignment. Each PLC team would administer the assessments in a similar timeframe and then share the result from each streamlined assessment to generate a more comprehensive understanding of student performance toward their shared curricular goals.

The teams realized that by collaboratively assessing their students, they could still gain a comprehensive view of student performance while cutting overall assessment time by more than 50 percent. Cara then worked with the teams to harness that saved time for small-group instruction based on assessment data.

COACHES COLLABORATION COORDINATION TOOL

You can use this collaboration coordination tool to identify opportunities for collaborative coaching. You can find a full-page version of this tool in the appendix or go to https://bit.ly/2ZiXqOf for an electronic version.

Directions: Reflect on the goals, interests, and responsibilities of the teachers with whom you work. List them in the appropriate column. Be brief in your descriptions. Once the form is filled out, you can sort it by any column to find collaboration opportunities.

Teacher	Goals	Interests	Responsibilities

TYPES OF COACH-FACILITATED COLLABORATIVE LEARNING

Now that you know how to identify appropriate collaborative groupings, it is time to explore various types of collaborative learning that can be vastly improved through coaching.

Book Talks: Book talks are one of the most common forms of self-guided professional learning. Sometimes book talks get a bad rap because they result in a lot of talking and not a lot of action. A coach's expertise can vastly benefit the process. A coach can use their expert questioning skills to engage all team members discussing the book. Coaches can also create the necessary follow-up plan to ensure the learning from the book talk is translated into improved instruction.

Data Reviews: There is no research-based best practice in education that can divide a group of teachers quite as profoundly as data-based instruction. You will often hear teachers proudly proclaim themselves as "data geeks" while others abashedly hide behind colleagues when they know the ensuing conversation will involve data. The unique perspective of an instructional coach can bridge this divide.

We must address the myth of the data-haves and the data-have-nots. In reality, most teachers rely on data. Some teachers prefer qualitative while others prefer quantitative data. Qualitative data examines human behavior while quantitative data examines numerical data. When teachers claim they are "data geeks," they are implying they are drawn to quantitative data. When teachers claim a distaste for data, they are saying they prefer qualitative data. Therefore, these teachers often suggest that the numbers and statistics so freely thrown around during educational discourse do not accurately portray the complete picture. They are correct! By combining qualitative and quantitative data results, we gain a more comprehensive and nuanced understanding of any situation.

Therein lies the coach's challenge. How can you bring together teachers' quantitative and qualitative perspectives to create a dynamic and collaborative opportunity? It is critical that you carefully consider the data you bring to the table. You can quickly turn off a substantial portion of the teachers you work with if you neglect quantitative or qualitative data. Ask yourself or, better yet, ask the teachers with whom you work, what information we would need to consider to understand the topic we will discuss most completely.

For example, you may be working with a group of Advanced Placement teachers who are poring over their high-stakes AP test results. Consider both the quantitative and qualitative data that could enhance the collaborative dialogue. Create a T-Chart and list some of the data that would likely be beneficial to the conversation. On one side, list the quantitative data that would represent the hard numbers and statistics with the power to inform the conversation. This could include the test results, a breakdown of those test results by demographic characteristics including gender, disability, or socioeconomic status, or a comparison of statistics from other districts or the state.

On the other side, include the qualitative data that will help you understand instructional choices that contribute to student success. This could include perceptual data collected from the students or teachers. Quick surveys work well for this sort of data collection. It could also include teacher reflections gathered as part of their PLC conversations.

As a coach, your role is to drive the team toward a more profound understanding. Again, rely on open-ended questions. You can use these questions to help teachers understand one another and their perspectives. These questions may also help a team understand more deeply what the data are saying. For instance, you may notice a discrepancy between male and female students receiving passing grades on their AP exams. You might point out this apparent discrepancy, but then follow up with an open-ended question about the qualitative data.

"Well, we can all see that boys seem to be outscoring girls on our AP stats exam. Is there anything in our qualitative data that could help us understand why this is occurring?" This sort of question links the qualitative and quantitative data to help teachers understand their mutual and interdependent benefit. Your job is to spark the conversation and back out, only reinserting yourself into the conversation when necessary. When the conversation reaches its natural conclusion, as noted by some tangible next steps, follow up with more reflective questions to reinforce the team's collaboration.

Lab Classrooms: Engaging in lab classrooms can inspire deep and meaningful learning. Lab classrooms consist of a teacher or team of teachers implementing some innovative instructional strategy while being observed by other teachers. Having a coach facilitate the lab classroom process will greatly enhance the outcome. Your first opportunity for coaching in a lab classroom is with the host teacher. It can be quite intimidating teaching on a stage while being observed by your colleagues. You could work with the host teacher to ensure they feel comfortable with the process.

Your next opportunity is to work with the observing teachers. You can guide them through a process of developing "look-fors" to ensure everyone fully understands the goals of the observation. You could also work with these teachers to hone their observation skills. Brainstorm all the ways they could gather data during this observation. Include taking notes of teaching behavior, interacting with students, gathering specific data such as comparing teacher talk to student talk time. What else might you include?

The real gold to be mined out of the lab classroom experience takes place when the entire team of teachers, including the host and observers, are in the same room to break down and analyze what they saw. This presents a rich collaborative opportunity to gain perspective that would be impossible from attending a workshop or reading a book. There is nothing like seeing exceptional teaching in action in your own school. Some examples of questions to ask in a lab classroom debrief could include:

- What evidence did you see of student engagement?
- What specific teaching strategies did you notice the host teacher use?
- What surprised you during the observation?
- How could we maximize the benefit of this strategy in our school?
- As your coach, how could I help you to be successful with this strategy?

CHAPTER REFLECTIONS

Are you a natural collaborator? Collaboration is one of the most challenging of the Five Thrive Factors as it ultimately depends on other people. Without your colleagues, there is no collaboration. Collaboration also presents some of the greatest potential to enhance not only your self-efficacy but the collective efficacy of your entire school. If you are a natural collaborator, continue to find ways to leverage your collaborative skills to continually support your self-efficacy. If collaborating with others is not your natural first choice, find small, nonthreatening ways to engage in this essential skill.

1. What are the first three words that come to mind when you think of professional collaboration?
2. How would you describe your collaborative habits?
3. Think of your favorite professional experience involving collaboration. How did the collaboration contribute to the success?
4. How did that experience impact your self-efficacy?
5. Think of a time when collaboration was not a positive experience. Why was that?
6. What conditions contribute to your ability to effectively collaborate with someone?

ACTION PLAN

In the last chapter, you reflected on how collaboration shapes who you are as a teacher. You previously wrote a short reflection about who you want to become as a teacher. How does collaboration fit into that vision? Consider where you are on the collaboration career stage continuum based on the results of the Thrive Inventory and your intuition. Where do you want to go, and who can help you get there? How can you harness the power of collaboration to move you toward that vision?

Maybe it is seeking a mentor who inspires you. Perhaps you want to engage in social media by joining professional networks. Maybe you are ready to serve as a coach to others, whether formally or informally. Once again, it is time for you to pledge one thing you will do to move toward that goal. Get that momentum going and just take that first step. It will be worth it!

10

Student Relationship Career Stages

When you travel, do you like to connect with the folks that live around your destination? Do you enjoy getting to know the people who work at your vacation hot spots? Many people find this sort of relationship-building enhances their travel experience. Some people take this very seriously and stay off the beaten path during their travels to ensure they have the opportunity to build authentic relationships. Relationships enhance any travel experience, including the journey you take while developing your teacher self-efficacy.

Thriving teachers go through a fascinating transition in the way they approach relationships with students. Think back to that exhilarating moment in every teacher's career when you were offered your first job. When you thought about the relationship you hoped to develop with your future students, where did your mind go? Now think of your favorite childhood teacher. Were there relationships you and your classmates had with this teacher similar to the way you imagined your relationships with your new students? For most thriving teachers, there is a significant difference between these two scenarios.

Early in a career, thriving teachers focus on developing positive relationships with each of their students. These relationships tend to manifest as friendships with students. As teachers progress into the mid-career stage, the focus of relationships shifts to a more strategic and results-based approach. In this stage, teachers focus on developing strong classroom communities where the relationship among students is equally as important as a relationship between the teacher and the students.

Thriving veteran teachers approach their relationships with students in a manner that more closely aligns with effective parenting strategies. At this stage, teachers find ways to leverage their positive relationships to push students beyond their comfort zones and develop their self-efficacy. Teachers tend to find this most elusive when considering the veteran development stage of all Five Thrive Factors. Strong student-teacher relationships contribute to students' safety and security in the school environment, increased sense of competence, and academic growth. For many veteran teachers, the ability to leverage the courage to expect more and push a little harder serves as the primary barrier to maximizing teacher self-efficacy. In this chapter, you will learn how to transition through these levels as you navigate your thriving professional journey.

	Teacher as Friend	Teacher as Community Developer	Teacher as Student Self-Efficacy Developer
Focus	Teacher-Focused	Class-Focused	Student-Focused
Style	Accommodating	Facilitating	Challenging
Approach	Reactive	Responsive	Proactive
Results	Disengagement	Engagement	Empowerment

Before you continue your exploration, it is once again time to pause and reflect on your Thriving Teacher Inventory results. Complete the table below with the corresponding results from the inventory. Now you can use these results to form your plan to lean into your student relationship skills as a self-efficacy boosting tool.

Student Relationships			
Stage 1: Friend	Stage 2: Community Builder	Stage 3: Student Efficacy Advocate	Total Self-Reflection Score

You will again use these results from the first part of the Thrive Inventory to help you guide your exploration through the rest of this book. The results can help determine which sections may be best suited for you. Your results above indicate your belief in your abilities to leverage student relationships to support your teacher self-efficacy. The individual scores for stages 1, 2, and 3 will indicate your proclivity to apply self-reflection at each stage.

The highest possible total score is 30. The total score is an informal measure of your student relationship efficacy. In other words, this total score indicates the belief you have in your ability to leverage collaboration to improve your practice. Consider the following scale as you reflect on your total score:

- 25-30: High relationship efficacy
- 19-24: Moderate relationship efficacy
- 13-18: Emerging relationship efficacy
- <13: Low relationship efficacy

Interpreting the scores for each level of student relationship development requires a refined approach. First, think about and reflect on the first stage, students as friends. The highest possible score for each stage is ten. A score of six or below indicates that focusing on developing friendly relationships with students may be an appropriate starting point. A score of seven or higher indicates a belief in your ability to leverage friendships with students and lets you know you should consider focusing on the higher levels.

STAGE 1: TEACHER AS FRIEND

When developing student relationships, teachers may cultivate friendships with students to demonstrate interest in their lives. In addition, teachers often view friendship with students as a foundational element to reaching more significant relationship-based goals. Although this is the earliest stage of student relationship development, viewing student relationships with a friendship lens is a valid and vital perspective.

Some teachers who develop friendships with students do so as a natural extension of their personality, often using humor to establish relationships. Other teachers strategically create these bonds to improve their effectiveness. The strategic approach to developing friendships can yield both social-emotional and academic benefits. The following three benefits are often cited by teachers who believe in the power of developing friendships with students:

1. Teachers who develop friendships with students allow students to see them as human and approachable. If students view a teacher as more approachable, they are more likely to seek assistance and ask questions. Think about this from your professional perspective. Which colleagues are you most likely to ask for assistance? For most teachers, the answer is those colleagues you feel are approachable and friendly. The same logic applies to students and their teachers.
2. When students view their teachers as friends, they can accelerate the process of lowering the anxiety of their students. Students are less likely to feel intimidated by teachers who are skilled at developing friendships. When students feel welcomed and enjoy spending time with their teachers, they can assuage some of the fears associated with the school. This lower anxiety can open the door to the final and most potentially durable of the three benefits.

3. Teachers who develop friendships with their students can promote productive risk-taking. When students view their teacher as more approachable, and their trepidation is decreased, they may seize opportunities that would otherwise feel too risky. Likewise, when students view their teachers as friendly allies, they are more likely to stretch themselves outside their comfort zones.

The issue is that there are significant risks in anchoring your relationships with students in terms of friendships. Overemphasizing friendships with some students can alienate other students. Just as kids and adults select their friends based on personal criteria, so do students with their teachers. It might be a little sad, but not all kids will like all of their teachers. If a student resists a friend-based relationship with their teacher, they can quickly become part of the out-crowd, while those that embrace the friendship find their social capital elevated. This dynamic works in opposition to the goals of a highly engaged egalitarian classroom community.

The teacher-student friendship dynamic can also detrimentally impact student behaviors. The in-crowd students who enjoy the positive attention from their teacher may become too comfortable and take advantage of the teacher's lackadaisical approach. However, the out-crowd students may rebel and increase their less-desirable behaviors. Either way, teachers must be incredibly careful to avoid overreliance on a friendship-based approach to building relationships.

CHARACTERISTICS OF TEACHER AS FRIEND

Teacher-Focused: Teachers who prioritize building relationships with students as friends are ultimately focused on their own needs. Teachers at this stage believe the only way to ensure relationships are solid is to have students like them. These teachers make the reasonable yet flawed assumption that being liked by students is facilitated only by creating a relationship that simulates the characteristics of student-to-student or, worse yet, adult-to-adult friendships.

New teachers can easily fall into the trap of overvaluing the desire to be liked by their students. There is a distinct difference between being liked and being friends. There certainly is room for this distinction without damaging a solid learning community with student voice and agency.

Accommodating: To accommodate is to alter practice to meet the wishes or desires of an individual or group. Healthy teacher accommodation focuses on meeting the actual needs of students. Teachers who assume an accommodating approach want to ensure their students are happy. This, of course, is not a bad thing. We all want our students to feel satisfied. Accommodating teachers use their friendship as the currency to drive their student relationships and happiness.

Teachers who operate as friends often adopt an overly accommodating style attempting to ensure students like them. This approach neglects the importance of the joy of learning and stresses the superficial happiness that students and teachers experience when they operate as friends. They accommodate the desires and whims of their students with the faulty assumption that students who like them will engage in the learning process. As a result, teachers accommodate the individual wants of each student instead of focusing on the needs of the overall learning community.

Over-accommodation is not a manifestation of empathy. Typically, it is an ingrained habit that rears its ugly head beyond the classroom and into other aspects of the over-accommodating teacher's life. Over-accommodating teachers are often over-accommodating colleagues, friends, and family members. This approach can result in teachers who frenetically bounce from relationship to relationship, trying to ensure everyone is happy instead of building mutually beneficial relationships built on trust and shared goals.

Reactive: Teachers focused on being friends with their students assume a reactive response. These teachers can become caged by the whims of their students. They give up their power in their quest to be liked. This approach trades the opportunity to build a highly functioning classroom community in exchange for the constant pursuit of the needs of each student in the classroom. Instead, they spend their relationship capital on short-term wins that serve individuals, not the community.

Disengagement: Unfortunately, focusing relationship-building capital on being friends with students results in disengagement. The students of teachers who base their relationships on being friends fall into one of three categories. They can end up in the productive in-crowd, the unproductive in-crowd, or the out-crowd. There is a significant risk of decreased engagement in all three of these categories.

The productive in-crowd is made up of students who feel that their teacher is their friend. They were able to remain focused on their work while not taking advantage of their teacher's friendly approach. This is a best-case scenario for students with teachers who focus on friendships. However, even though these students can maintain appropriate boundaries and engage in the expected learning experiences, they are still limited because they cannot fully engage with all other members of the classroom community who may not fall into this category.

Students in the unproductive in-crowd have achieved the status of "popular kid" among their classmates. As a result, they take advantage of their teacher's friendly approach and begin placing unreasonable demands on their teacher and classmates. For example, a student in the unproductive in-crowd may seek attention by engaging in sarcastic banter with their teacher, whom they view as a peer. This disrupts the learning environment and creates more barriers between student groups, thus eroding the potential of a highly functioning classroom community.

Students in the out-crowd suffer the worst fate in a classroom led by a teacher who overrelies on their friendships with students. Students in the out-crowd do not see their teacher as their friend. Instead, they perceive their teacher as a friend of other students in the class. This places students in the out-crowd in an incredibly emotionally vulnerable position, feeling like they're segregated from their classmates and their teacher. When students feel distanced from their teacher, they can become disengaged entirely and lack the typical recourse of working with their teacher to reengage.

STAGE 2: TEACHER AS CLASSROOM COMMUNITY CREATOR

A classroom is not just a room full of children with a few adults sprinkled in. A classroom truly is a community. A community is characterized by shared goals, attitudes, and cultural norms. A strong community requires a sense of collective commitment to the success of all members resulting in a productive fellowship.

Classroom community is no different from any other community. Strong classroom communities support improved social and academic learning for all students. A thriving classroom community is an essential component of any student-centric learning environment. Teachers who view their role related to developing relationships with students as classroom community creators offer a beautiful gift to their students who achieve their academic goals and learn how to support and be supported by others.

CHARACTERISTICS OF TEACHER AS COMMUNITY CREATOR

Class Focused: It does not take long for most teachers to realize they need to shift from being a friend with all of their students. The next step in developing relationships with students is to focus on creating a strong classroom community. As teachers shift from a friend to a classroom community creator, they more efficiently focus their energies on the entire class instead of each student.

Teachers at this stage develop engagement strategies and learning experiences that build a bond among students. For example, teachers at this stage often used a goal-setting ceremony to cement relationships and develop a collective commitment to all students' success. Teachers facilitate a process through which all students share their long-term aspirations. They then translate these long-term aspirations into annual goals. Each student shares their goals while the rest of the class considers how they can support their classmate in the quest to meet their goals. Skilled teachers at this stage leverage these goals to create classroom norms by reflecting on the sort of classroom necessary for all students to accomplish their goals.

Facilitating: Teachers at this stage employ a facilitative style empowering the classroom community to develop into a network of learners committed to the success of all members of the learning community. Teachers who act as facilitators elevate the voices of their students. They step outside of their role of the dominant voice in the class and find ways to amplify the students' voices.

Teachers who are exceptionally skilled as facilitators commit to learning about their students as individuals. They take a very personalized approach to developing relationships. They cannot be friends with their students, but they can find ways to connect students with the resources they need to succeed, including other students. These teachers strategically group students to leverage their shared and unique talents. They create networks where students can take risks, fail forward, and uncover their talents and passions.

Responsive: Teachers at this stage assume a responsive approach to building relationships and creating classroom community. Responsive Classroom, a leader in professional learning around social-emotional learning and classroom community, defines classroom community as "a safe, predictable, joyful, and inclusive environment."[1] Responsive teachers know how to build relationships with students that create a vibrant and engaging learning environment designed to respond to all students' developmental, social, and academic needs.

The root word of responsive is obviously "respond." To be responsive is to respond proactively, when possible, quickly when necessary, and appropriately always. A responsive student-teacher relationship allows teachers to consider each student in the class as an individual while fostering relationships that will encourage student agency. A responsive relationship is predicated on good timing. A responsive teacher knows when to provide structure and guidance and when to back away and let students take charge in their interpersonal relationship development.

Engagement: The long-term result of this approach is student engagement. The ideal learning environment is built by teachers who focus on developing a classroom community sense of safety and belonging. Recent research suggests that student engagement consists of behavioral, emotional, cognitive, and agential aspects. By leveraging strong relationships to build classroom community, teachers can enhance all four elements of student engagement.

A strong classroom community allows students to invest in the behavioral expectations of the classroom. Students can view the classroom norms as a support for the success of all as opposed to an adult-imposed compliance tool. Strong relationships designed to promote community engender a sense of emotional safety. A vibrant classroom community encourages healthy risk-taking allowing for academic and cognitive growth. Finally, by engaging all students in the development of the classroom community, student agency is bolstered by empowering all students to generate a sense of ownership in their learning.

STAGE 3: TEACHER AS STUDENT SELF-EFFICACY DEVELOPER

As we have learned throughout this book, thriving teachers have high levels of teacher self-efficacy. It stands to reason that thriving students also have high levels of self-efficacy. At the most advanced stage of relationship building, thriving teachers leverage their relationships to bolster their students' self-efficacy.

This approach to building student relationships is unique in that it intentionally makes students uncomfortable, which, to some, seems contrary to the concept of building relationships. Take a moment to think about teachers who had a positive impact on your life. If you are like most, you will think of someone who believed in you and challenged you to dig deep and be more than even you thought you could be. This does not work without a trusting relationship. This is the essence of a student self-efficacy developer.

CHARACTERISTICS OF STUDENT SELF-EFFICACY DEVELOPER

Student-Focused: Teachers at this stage are genuinely student-focused in their relationship building. They have already learned how to form friendly relationships, and they consistently build highly functioning classroom communities as an ordinary course of their work. This opens opportunities to focus their relationship building on the needs of each student. They consider the hopes and dreams of each of their students. They find ways to challenge and inspire all students as individuals and as important learning community members.

Thriving teachers at this career stage personalize their approach and strive to build a trusting relationship with each student, knowing that relationship building is not a one-size-fits-all endeavor. Instead, they consider each student's strengths, needs, skills, and interests and develop specific plans to support their individual development.

Challenging: Teachers at this stage begin to question their students beyond their current comfort zones. This challenging style most aptly defines this stage in relationship building. Teachers at this stage realize they must leverage their efforts in building relationships to foster student growth so as not to squander their hard work. Thriving teachers at this stage ask the tough questions and expect more from their students, understanding that the relationships they have developed allow students to accept and appreciate the challenge.

Teachers at this stage strive to increase their student agency in their learning. They want their students to take responsibility for their learning by setting rigorous goals and overcoming obstacles to reach those goals. The teacher approaches their craft like a coach, supporting when necessary and challenging when possible. As students rise to the challenge and learn that they have more potential than they realized, their self-efficacy increases.

Proactive: This is the most proactive approach teachers can take related to student relationships. They are laser-focused on the long-term success of their students. They certainly carry forward their responsive tendencies from the previous stage, but they include more forethought and planning in the process. They do not present haphazard challenges to their students. Instead, they strategically find ways to challenge their students based on careful planning and personalization.

Empowerment: The long-term implementation of this approach leads to student empowerment. Students fortunate enough to have teachers skilled in the art of student self-efficacy development enjoy increased confidence and resilience. They learn to challenge themselves and find ways to embrace the hurdles that inevitably dot the path toward any worthy goal. These teachers generate enhanced student agency and increased student self-efficacy.

STUDENT RELATIONSHIPS AND THE FOUR DOMAINS OF TEACHER SELF-EFFICACY

Once again, it is time to explore the four domains of teacher self-efficacy. Take a look at the factor of student relationships. How do the student relationships you work so hard to maintain impact your self-efficacy in the four domains of instruction, engagement, classroom community, and self-care?

The student relationship factor is directly linked to the classroom community domain. Teachers build classroom community self-efficacy by forming strong relationships among themselves and their students, and among their students as a community. This is not to suggest solid student relationships do not impact the other three domains of self-efficacy.

Perhaps strong relationships allow you to bolster your instructional self-efficacy because you can challenge students and push just a little bit harder. After all, they trust you. You could boost your engagement self-efficacy because your students become increasingly engaged as you strengthen your relationships with them. This same action could positively impact your classroom community self-efficacy. You could also support your self-care efficacy by creating a caring and interdependent classroom. We must never forget we are part of our classroom community, not outside observers.

Take a moment to jot down your scores to remind you where you may want to focus your energies. As you contemplate the impact student relationships could have on your self-efficacy, keep in mind these four domains. Think about your connection between student relationships and the four domains and use that information to guide your professional learning.

CHARTING YOUR STUDENT RELATIONSHIP PATHWAY

Strong student relationships form the basis for every triumph teachers experience. Teachers do what they do because they care deeply about students.

- Based on what you have read and your results from the Thrive Inventory, how would you describe your current stage of student relationship development?

As you consider the progression from one stage to the next on the student relationship continuum, keep in mind the Focus and Influence Model. This model explains how the path from one stage to the next in any of the Five Thrive Factors is fueled by a refined focus on students or expanding influence. As we will see in the following sections, both focus and influence can propel the progression from each stage to the next, but in some cases, one of the sources of fuel is more evident and direct.

MAXIMIZING POSITIVE RELATIONSHIPS

Take some time to think about your friends. Who was your best childhood friend? Picture yourself as a child spending time with that friend. Now picture one of your best current friends. What traits do both of these friends share? What does it mean to you to be a good friend? When others have been asked these questions, a few common themes emerged. How closely do these themes match your list?

- Fun
- Trusting and trustworthy
- Supportive
- Loyal
- Sense of humor
- Honest; even with tough messages
- Dependable
- Nonjudgmental
- Good listener

These are beautiful traits for which to strive. Exercising these traits will not draw you into any of the pitfalls of an overreliance on teachers as friends. A typical interview question for teachers is whether the candidate wants to be liked or respected. Although this question creates a false dichotomy, the answer to this question can be telling. The generally assumed correct answer is more emphasis should be given to respect, but we must not assume these are opposite ends of a continuum. Most good teachers are liked and respected by the majority of their students.

The problems arise in the teacher-student friendship when boundaries are disrespected. However, you can follow a few guidelines to ensure your friendships with students are still mutually respectful and productive. The first guideline is to ensure your relationships encourage students to adhere to the classroom norms. The second guideline is to ensure all students have a voice in the classroom. The third and final guideline is to examine the power dynamics in the classroom and ensure they contribute to the success of all members of the learning community.

First, ensure your friendly relationships encourage students to follow the class norms. If you notice students decrease their adherence to the class norms, they may be taking advantage of your friendships. Friends tend to tolerate more from one another than they would from colleagues. Friends are not likely to establish norms and expectations for their relationship. If you maintain friendly relationships with students and see pro-social behaviors increase and firm adherence to class norms, you likely have set up positive friendly relationships.

Second, you want to ensure all students have a voice in the class. Be certain a few student voices are not taking over due to their privileged status as teacher's friends. You can use the "How Well Do I Know My Students?" tool to ensure you are hearing all of your students. Create a three-column sheet of paper or spreadsheet (see appendix for a fillable form or go to https://bit.ly/3DUc0uI for an interactive version). List your students in the first column as they come to your mind. Avoid alphabetical order or a seating chart. Just print the names as they come to mind. In the middle column, write one thing you know the child genuinely enjoys. In the third column, indicate with a checkmark if you are certain the student knows you know this about them. The results of this analysis will quickly provide you with an accounting of the students with whom you share the most substantial personal connection.

How would you respond if you found it difficult to remember a student? What if you could not think of something about which a student is especially passionate? Are there students for whom you found it especially easy to identify passions? How do their classmates perceive those students? These questions are all judgment-free. They are intended to help you identify the positive aspects of your friendships with your students and any potential pitfalls.

The final guideline you can use to ensure that your friendships with students are positive and contribute to the success of your entire classroom community is to heed the power dynamics in your classroom. In any classroom environment, specific individuals wield more social capital than others. This social capital can serve as an excellent tool for promoting pro-social behavior and a strong classroom community. It also, however, can divide the classroom and create haves and have-nots. Therefore, it is imperative that you pay attention to these social dynamics to empower silenced voices and guide dominant voices to use their social capital for the good of all.

Careful observation allows you to examine these relationships and power dynamics. Unfortunately, it is very challenging to find the time to observe your class due to the demands of your time as a teacher. If you have access to an instructional coach, ask them to watch your class with some specific guidance about the power dynamics you seek to understand. You could also ask the coach to cover your teaching responsibilities to allow you to conduct such an observation. Consider collecting data about each interaction between your students and assess the positivity and the influence of each interaction. For each interaction rate the positivity on the following scale:

- −3 = Extremely Negative (i.e., bullying behavior)
- −2 = Negative (i.e., teasing)
- −1 = Slightly Negative (i.e., ignoring)
- 0 = Neutral (i.e., casual conversation)
- 1 = Slightly Positive (i.e., including others)
- 2 = Positive (i.e., encouraging)
- 3 = Extremely Positive (i.e., standing up for someone else)

Then rate each interaction for its influence. When any interaction takes place in a social setting, it can have various degrees of influence. If the influence is low, it barely registers with the people directly involved. To be fair, this is rare, and a dangerous assumption as social interactions usually impact those involved to a greater degree than others would assume. However, if the influence is strong, others in the community can mimic the behavior, whether the observed behavior is negative or positive. Rate these on a simple 3-point scale, with 1 being low influence and 3 being high influence. Make both of these evaluations quickly and base your score on your initial intuition.

Collect this data during experiences where students can freely work with many classmates either individually or as part of a team. Do not overthink your ratings to ensure you can collect many data points. When you analyze the data, you are looking for positive and negative trends. If you see a positive trend coupled with high influence, strategize ways to replicate that trend. If you see a positive and low influence trend, find ways to amplify the students' voices to increase their influence. If you see a negative trend with low influence, see if you can redirect toward positivity.

The most concerning apparent trend is a negative one with high influence. You might see this as a popular student who has considerable political capital who treats their classmates disrespectfully. These behaviors can spread like a virus in a classroom-based on friendships between teachers and students. If you have too many of these sorts of influences, your classroom community will need some retooling.

In these instances, it is critical to meet with the students individually and share your observations. Try to help these students see how they can alter their behavior while still maintaining their social capital but using it to benefit the classroom community. Classroom meetings focused on the topic of influence can also be helpful. However, be very careful not to alienate the students with whom you are directly working by making them feel blamed.

In general, use the data to accentuate positive trends and mitigate negative trends. Just remember, it is good to be friendly with your students, but your role as a teacher must transcend superficial friendships. Your job is to facilitate social, emotional, and academic growth for all your students. Sometimes being friendly helps you achieve these goals; sometimes being a friend is not enough.

MOVING TOWARD CLASSROOM-COMMUNITY BUILDER

Shifting the focus of your relationship-building from friend to community builder can be one of the most transformational shifts you make in your career. This shift occurs relatively soon for most thriving teachers and is often spurred by experiencing some of the pitfalls of operating as a friend. By focusing on developing classroom community, you significantly increase your capacity to meet your students' needs by including all class members in the process.

Building a sense of classroom community is often relegated to the realm of classroom management, but it is so much more than that. While it is undoubtedly true that developing a strong classroom community contributes to a productive and positive learning environment, these goals are accomplished through empowerment rather than control. You can transform your relationships from friend to community builder by focusing on the following shifts in perspective and approach.

Focus on trust over fun. Classroom communities rely on trust. There must be trust between you and your students and among your students. Your students develop trust in you when they know they can count on you for doing what you have said. Students must trust you will be fair and put their interests at the heart of your decision-making. Once trust has been established, students will more readily find joy in their learning as they pursue their passions. When students develop trust in you and their classmates, they will begin to see how much you care.

Shift from making things comfortable to making things relevant. It is natural for a student to request accommodations or support to make things easier. Resist the temptation to give in to these requests. Instead, consider making the learning more relevant to the student requesting a more straightforward path when receiving these requests. Connect the learning to the students' aspirations or the aspirations of other members of the learning community. Listen for the "why" behind their request. Perhaps they are providing indirect feedback implying they are not finding relevance in the learning experience. There are a lot of correct answers to the question, "Why do we need to know this?" One answer that is certainly wrong is "Because I said so." It is our job to make sure the learning is relevant.

Remember, play is not just for fun. Being playful and engaging in meaningful games provides far more than entertainment. Play can help students develop social and emotional competencies, as well as strengthen the classroom community, if it is well designed and purposeful. If the games you are designing are competitive, make sure the competition is friendly. When you are in the early stages of developing classroom community, focus on cooperative games that do not result in winners and losers. You can increase the level of competition when you know you have a vigorous and supportive classroom community.

Shift from monologue to dialogue. Teachers often engage in too much teacher talk in a classroom with relationships based on friendships with students. Sometimes the excessive teacher talk is driven by the desire to entertain. Other times, it is caused by the classroom's dependence on step-by-step teacher guidance. Engaging your students in meaningful dialogue and discussion can strengthen their sense of student agency, resulting in a stronger sense of ownership over their learning.

LEVERAGING RELATIONSHIPS FOR STUDENT SELF-EFFICACY

Leveraging relationships for student self-efficacy is not an alternative to building classroom community. It is an extension. When you have developed a strong classroom community, students enjoy 360-degree support. You support them directly as their teacher, and they receive support from the groups with whom they work and all of their classmates. With all that support, you can find opportunities to increase their self-efficacy by stretching them outside of their comfort zones.

Getting students out of their comfort zones is critical as it guarantees they will engage in new experiences and find more opportunities. In addition, if they trust you and their classmates, they know they can take risks without the fear of experiencing humiliation if the attempt is not perfect.

You can follow this five-step process for nudging students outside their comfort zones by leveraging your vital relationships.

1. *Connect to their Passions:* At this point, you will have identified the hopes and dreams of your students. You want to draw a connection between your students' passions and the areas in which you want to challenge them. For example, a student has identified a desire to be the first member of their family to attend a four-year university. You notice the student has a hesitancy to speak up in class. You could challenge them to practice their public speaking skills and address the student body at an upcoming assembly.
2. *Stretch to Identify the Big Picture:* In this step, you want to stretch your students' perspectives so they can see their big picture goals and the value of stepping outside their comfort zones. Encourage them to see themselves in that desired state. Help them imagine the whole sensory experience related to the success. Let them know you will support them, but the hard work of achieving this goal is theirs.
3. *Challenge to Identify Barriers:* Now it is time to identify the barriers that get in the way of achieving the big picture goal. This can be emotionally challenging as the barriers often run deep. This is where you will genuinely be leveraging the relationships you have developed. You want them to know you are there to support them while encouraging them to face their inner demons.
4. *Balance Social, Emotional, and Academic Variables:* In any big picture goal for students, there are likely social, emotional, and academic elements of meeting the goal. There are also expected social, emotional, and academic barriers. Balancing all of these variables is an art in and of itself. You need to learn when to push, when to support, when to focus on social and emotional aspects, and when to focus on academic aspects. There is no simple recipe to mastering this step. It is entirely dependent on the relationship you have with each of your students. There is a reason why this is the final stage in the student relationship theme.
5. *Chart the Path:* The final step is to chart the course by setting small achievable goals and helping students meet their goals. You want to help your student muster the grit to feel responsible for meeting the goal. They must know it is not your goal, but you are there to offer support. Then, when they meet their goal, feel free to celebrate like it was your own! You deserve it because you gave this student the beautiful gift of increased self-efficacy.

COACH'S CORNER

A coach's role in support of strong relationships among teachers and students can be advantageous. Coaches are exceptionally skilled in making the unseen seen. Unfortunately, the relationships teachers have with their students often fall into the unrecognized category. As a coach, you can help teachers gain perspective and understanding related to their relationships with students.

High-quality coaching is based on effective questioning. Using open-ended questions is especially helpful when exploring something as complex and intricate as interpersonal relationships. We will explore three scenarios and some related questions. Each scenario describes a teacher looking to progress through the developmental career stages of student relationship development.

SCENARIO #1

Consider a new teacher in her first three years of teaching who wants to be friends with her students and is losing control of the classroom. Imagine this teacher's principal suggested some professional development about "classroom management." Upon initial observation, you recognize the friend-based relationships seem to be getting in the way of leading an effective learning environment. Here are some questions and prompts to consider:

- How would you describe an effective learning environment?
- How would you describe your learning environment?
- Would you rather be liked or respected?
- With which students do you feel you have the best relationship?
- How would they describe you?
- With which students do you feel your relationship could use some work?
- How would they describe you?
- What are your thoughts about your classroom community?
- Would you be open to partnering on strengthening your classroom community?

SCENARIO #2

Imagine a well-liked veteran teacher, who has a reputation of developing highly effective classroom communities, reaches out because she has a few students whom she feels are complacent. Once you observe this teacher, you are impressed by how her students interact with her and one another. You realize she could cash in some of her relational capital to nudge students outside their comfort zones.

- How would you describe your relationship with your students?
- How did you go about developing the classroom community you have?

- How would you describe your teacher self-efficacy?
- How would you describe the self-efficacy of your students?
- How do you challenge your students to do more than they believe they can?
- Could we partner with some student goal setting and efficacy work with your students?

SCENARIO #3

Consider a veteran teacher who believes his students lack respect because they are noncompliant at times. This teacher is looking for classroom management strategies to regain control of his classroom. When you observe him, you notice a tremendous amount of teacher talk and students primarily working independently. You also notice his interactions with students are generally positive, if not somewhat cold.

- How would you describe your relationships with students?
- What does the perfect classroom look like?
- What are your goals for student engagement?
- In what sort of settings do you learn best?
- Have you asked your students how they learn best?
- Do you know what your students hope and dream for?
- What do you hope for them?
- Could we try a little exercise? (At this point, you could use the "How Well Do You Know Your Students?" activity.)
- Could we work on some strategies to continue to develop your classroom community?

Just as the relationships among teachers and students are very complex, so are the relationships between coach and teacher. When working on something as delicate as interpersonal relationships with students, forge your path forward based on your relationships with your teachers. Your work is critical and can lead to a gift for countless students by facilitating a process toward improved relationships.

CHAPTER REFLECTIONS

1. How do you know when you have developed a strong relationship with a student?
2. Have you ever struggled to form a relationship with a particular student?
3. If so, how did that make you feel?
4. How did you respond?
5. Think back to a student with whom you had a particularly positive relationship. What made that relationship strong?
6. What lessons could you learn from that relationship?

ACTION PLAN

In this chapter, you explored the complex and beautiful landscape of relationships. The three stages of student relationships for thriving teachers include teacher as a friend, teacher as a classroom-community creator, and teacher as student self-efficacy developer. As you consider your action plan, remember these stages are all positive. Our students deserve friendly teachers, strong classroom communities, and self-efficacy advocates. Challenge yourself to pledge one thing you will do to move toward a goal of refined relationships with students. The time is now. Small steps add up quickly!

11
Inclusive Practice Career Stages

We conclude our exploration of the Thrive Factors by examining inclusion. Inclusion is the direct and profound result of elevated levels of the individual teacher and collective efficacy. When a school community shares a commitment to providing a world-class education to all kids and believes it has the skills to deliver, transformation occurs. When teachers implement inclusive practices and succeed, their self-efficacy blossoms. Inclusion catalyzes self-efficacy by directly demonstrating to teachers that they have the skills to excel for all kids.

No self-respecting traveler embarks on their journey without a good camera. As you consider your own teacher self-efficacy career journey, imagine you have a magic camera. When you look through this camera at a group of students, only the students you believe you can reach appear in your viewfinder. When you press the orange Engagement button, you only see those you believe you can engage. When you press the green Instruction button, you only see those for whom you feel you can effectively provide meaningful instruction. When you press the blue Classroom Community button, you only see those students who are active participants in your classroom community. When you press the purple Self-Care button, you take a selfie indicating how well you can give yourself grace in your current classroom climate or school culture.

Think of the Thriving Teacher Model as a model of this magic camera through which you could view your classes. As you look through the concentric circles at all of your students, you can evaluate your level of efficacy for each domain. In an idealized state, you could look through your magic camera at your class and see every student every day. When you take the selfie, you see yourself as always equipped to take care of yourself and engage in strategies allowing you to remain resilient in the face of challenges.

When you look at the model below, you can think of this as a graphic organizer of your magic camera. The further you are toward the outside ring in each section, the more efficacious you feel. Additionally, the further you are toward the outside ring, the more inclusive you will be. There is a beautiful cycle at play here. The more efficacious you are, the more inclusive you will be, and the more inclusive you are, the more efficacious you will become. That is magic!

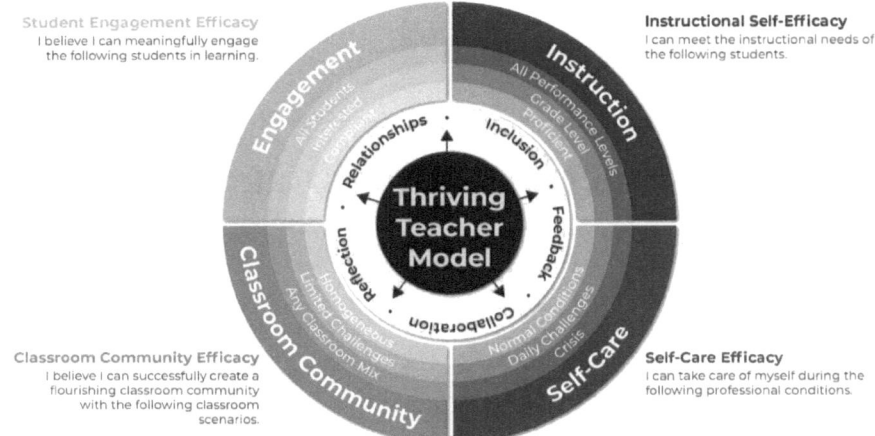

Thriving Teacher Model. David Grambow. *Thriving Teacher Model*. 2021.

	Experimenting	**Implementing**	**Leading**
Focus	Professional Learning	Student Learning	Professional and Student Learning
Approach	Casual	Formal	Transformational
Results	Teacher Self-Efficacy	Teacher and Student Self-Efficacy	Collective Efficacy

Now you can complete the final table below with the corresponding results from the inventory. This is the final element of your thriving journey plan that will allow you to leverage the power of embracing inclusive practices as a self-efficacy enhancer.

Inclusive Practices			
Stage 1: Experimenting	**Stage 2: Implementing**	**Stage 3: Leading**	**Total Self-Reflection Score**

The results from the first part of the Thrive Inventory will help you guide your exploration. These results can help you determine which sections of the book may be most pertinent to your set of circumstances, dispositions, and habits. Your results above indicate your belief in your abilities to leverage inclusion as a tool to enhance your teacher self-efficacy. The individual scores for stages 1, 2, and 3 will indicate your proclivity to access inclusive practices at each stage.

The highest possible total score is 30. The total score is an informal measure of your inclusion efficacy. In other words, this total score indicates the belief you have in your ability to leverage collaboration to improve your practice. Consider the following scale as you reflect on your total score:

25–30: High inclusive efficacy
19–24: Moderate inclusive efficacy
13–18: Emerging inclusive efficacy
<13: Low inclusive efficacy

Remember to think about and reflect on the first stage, experimenting with inclusive practices. The highest possible score for each stage is ten. A score of six or below indicates that experimenting with inclusive practices could be an area for growth and focus. A score of seven or higher indicates a strong belief in your ability to experiment with inclusion and suggests you should consider strategies at the higher levels.

STAGE 1: EXPERIMENTING WITH INCLUSIVE PRACTICES

Inclusive practices are firmly rooted in a philosophical stance asserting all students deserve a meaningful educational experience with their peers. At the experimenting stage, teachers are beginning to explore their understanding of this philosophical stance. Teachers at this stage increase the inclusive capacity of a school system. Their experimentation generates ideas and dialogue about those ideas.

Teachers at this experimenting stage of inclusive practices focus on their professional learning. They take a casual approach to their experimentations with inclusive practices. These efforts result in the development of individual teacher self-efficacy. As you read the descriptions below, ask yourself how these characteristics relate to your inclusive practices and preferences.

CHARACTERISTICS OF EXPERIMENTING WITH INCLUSIVE PRACTICES

Professional Learning: Experimenting with inclusive practices is a wonderful source of personalized professional learning. Curiosity and creativity spur open-mindedness and broadened perspectives. The challenges of providing more inclusive services to students inspire teachers to employ their creativity to meet this challenge head-on. They increase their professional toolkit of inclusive practices through a process of trial and error.

Teachers at this stage also advance the professional learning of their colleagues. Often it takes teachers at this stage to shake off some of the rust in a school system by thinking outside the box. They are not afraid to try something new. When colleagues see teachers at this stage finding success, they can translate these isolated practices into a more systematized approach. The interdependence of teachers at various stages in developing their inclusive practice serves as a great example of the importance of diverse teams of teachers with different backgrounds, styles, and years of experience.

Casual: Teachers at this stage approach their inclusive practices casually. This is not to suggest they do not take inclusion seriously. They simply are willing to try strategies separate from any formal structure or system. Fortunately, preservice teacher programs have improved their curriculum around inclusion. New teachers are entering the profession with a deeper understanding of the importance of inclusive education. They accept the challenge as a matter of course and are accordingly more willing to experiment casually.

Teacher Self-Efficacy: If teachers at this stage continue to experiment with inclusive practices and land on a few strategies that work, the result is an increase in their self-efficacy. Nothing breeds success like success. When a novice teacher finds more students achieving success in their classroom with a decrease in segregated services, they develop a sense of pride and accomplishment, inviting further experimentation.

Think back to your own early teaching experiences. Was there a time when you found you had "the magic touch" with a student who previously faced challenges keeping them from inclusively participating with their peers? How did it feel? What did you do differently allowing students to succeed? How did this inform your future practices?

STAGE 2: IMPLEMENTING INCLUSIVE PRACTICES

Like most thriving teachers in the mid-career stage, your previous experimentations with inclusive practices led you to implement certain practices into your everyday instructional and community-building routines. Teachers at this stage have learned what works for them and what does not work for them via experimentation. They now winnow and sift through their experiments creating a style all their own.

Teachers at this implementing stage of inclusive practices focus on their students' learning. They adopt a more formal approach to their experimentations with inclusive practices. Their inclusive efforts result in further development of their teacher self-efficacy and an increase in student self-efficacy. Have you moved from experimenting to implementing inclusive practices? How did this transition feel, and how did it impact your beliefs about inclusion?

CHARACTERISTICS OF IMPLEMENTING INCLUSIVE PRACTICES

Student Learning: Teachers at the implementing stage of inclusion focus on proven strategies to impact student learning by creating an environment where more students can learn with their peers. These teachers consider the needs of all of their students and develop specific plans for each student to find success. They realize inclusion is not about a place; it is about a sense of belonging that can only be achieved when all structures and systems are proactively created with all students in mind.

The personalized learning movement embodies the concept of proactively and deliberately implementing inclusive practices. Personalization is based on the customization of instruction and learning experiences to provide each child with what they need to succeed. There have been countless examples of personalized learning implemented with great success where student voice and choice informed the learning of all students. Unfortunately, there are just as many examples of attempted personalized learning implementation lowering the bar for students and resulting in watered-down expectations by creating a free-for-all.

Personalized learning and inclusion must be implemented thoughtfully with measurable goals for all students. If done correctly, all students can more deeply engage in the learning experiences, increase their student agency, and, ultimately, learn at higher levels. When developing personalized learning plans for all students in an inclusive setting, you must consider the standards, your students' readiness, their passions and interests, and their motivators. Consider a student who you would like to find more success in your classroom. How could taking a more personalized approach to their learning open the door both literally and figuratively to their success in your classroom?

Formal: Teachers at this level take a more formal approach to their implementation strategies related to inclusion. They become more systematic with an eye on consistency and results. Fidelity to the strategy rises in importance as teachers at this stage realize structure and consistency yield improved equitable results. These teachers focus their energy on processes and procedures they can easily replicate consistently.

For example, teachers at this stage might create systems where they meet with the families of their students a few weeks before the school year starts to find out more about the hopes and dreams of the child and their family. They may also meet with all service providers including special educators, gifted and talented teachers, and interventionists on a regular basis to co-plan for student success. It might look like a special educator who puts extra time into establishing a student's strengths as an integral part of their IEP and then finds ways to leverage those strengths in their general education classroom. What examples have you seen?

Teacher and Student Self-Efficacy: Teachers at this stage improve their teacher self-efficacy; they also increase the students' self-efficacy in their class. The tremendous benefit of improving student self-efficacy occurs in two ways. First and most directly, students learn they can be successful in their class with their peers. The time students are segregated decreases. Student self-efficacy increases by engaging in mastery experiences and social modeling, two of Bandura's identified sources.

Second, many students indirectly increase their self-efficacy by working with teachers who consistently implement inclusive practices. Inclusion benefits students who would not have received instruction in segregated settings regardless of the teachers' use of inclusive practices. Well-crafted instruction in an inclusive and heterogeneous classroom allows students to reframe their understanding of content by engaging in learning experiences with classmates with varied levels of understanding and perspectives. When students have the opportunity to reexamine and reflect on their understanding, their confidence and self-efficacy benefit. The key is deliberate planning focused on the learning of all students.

STAGE 3: LEADING SYSTEMIC INCLUSION

Thriving teachers at the most advanced stage in their inclusive practice development lead systemic inclusion. The experimentation and implementation of inclusive strategies set the stage for teachers to step into leadership roles. After teachers realize the positive, and in some cases transformational, impact of their inclusive practices, they feel compelled to share the good news through leadership. This leadership manifests in several ways, including advocacy, collaborative engagement, and influential leadership.

Many teachers at this stage emerge as leaders for inclusion through their advocacy and modeling. They engage in conversation with colleagues and district leaders sharing their passion for inclusion while contributing to moving initiatives forward. These teachers feed their self-efficacy through expanding their influence with a goal of increased inclusion.

For others, they find ways to collaboratively engage with others who are leading the inclusive charge. They may join committees focused on inclusion or elevate their professional learning teams to focus on inclusion. Later, you will learn about Rigor Teamwork Inclusion, a framework allowing for this sort of collaborative engagement at a district level.

Some teachers choose to take their message to the streets and exercise their influential leadership skills. These teachers beat the drum whenever the opportunity arises. They relentlessly share their message about the importance of inclusion as a moral imperative. All of these leadership avenues enhance self-efficacy and create opportunities for inclusion to flourish.

CHARACTERISTICS OF ADVOCATING FOR INCLUSIVE PRACTICES

Professional and Student Learning: Teachers at this stage in their inclusive practices focus on professional learning and student learning. The work of developing others results in professional learning. When advocacy results in improved practices, student learning improves. The passion and purpose driving professional learning can result in transformational change where teams do and see things differently.

Can you think of a time when someone inspired you to take a more inclusive approach? Have you ever been the one to inspire others to implement an inclusive strategy? How would you describe those experiences? How would you describe the learning that occurred?

Transformational: Teachers at this stage take a transformational approach to their inclusive practices. You have seen the term "transformational" a few times in this book. What does transformational really mean? Transformational leadership results in a significant change in perspective and long-lasting changes in practice. It tends to generate broader and more inclusive perspectives considering multiple viewpoints. Teachers at this stage set out deliberately to disrupt the status quo and change their school or district for the better.

For example, a teacher at this stage may advocate for a co-teaching model for all students receiving reading intervention at their elementary school. Through her advocacy, she could build a coalition of like-minded colleagues who then build a system allowing for a fully inclusive reading support program. Her approach, in this case, changed not just practice but also hearts and minds. Transformation is only possible with aspiration and collaboration.

Collective Efficacy: The net result of leading for inclusion is what John Hattie has identified as the number one variable positively impacting student achievement: collective efficacy. Collective efficacy is a team's shared belief in their abilities and skills to accomplish their goals. In the realm of education, collective efficacy is the sense a school staff has in their abilities to meet the needs of the students for whom they share responsibility.

Leadership for inclusion generates collective efficacy by inspiring the development of systems designed to reach all students. Teachers everywhere want to do everything they can to inspire and support their students to maximize their potential. Sometimes their perceived barriers to achieving this reside outside their control. If a collaborative team can create systems aligned with the efforts of the entire team, school, or even district, they can remove the perceived barriers. With those barriers removed, teams will have the support and systems to implement inclusive practices, generating self-efficacy. This is the beauty of the cyclical and interdependent nature of the Thrive Factors. They all work together, aligning their efforts, strengthening their shared belief as a staff, and, ultimately, manifesting the benefits of great teachers and excellent schools.

INCLUSION AND THE FOUR DOMAINS OF TEACHER SELF-EFFICACY

Inclusion stands apart from the four other Thrive Factors when you consider the relationship to the four domains of self-efficacy. High levels of self-efficacy definitively result in an inclusive mindset. When you feel efficacious, you are more likely to embrace the unique challenges presented by your students as opportunities. If you are faced with students who require specialized instruction, and you have elevated levels of instructional efficacy, you are likely to implement strategies to allow the students to be successful in your classroom. The same logic applies to classroom community efficacy and student engagement efficacy.

Research overwhelmingly supports inclusive practices as the best long-term strategy for success for all students. Possessing an inclusive mindset can readily boost self-efficacy in the three domains previously mentioned. Your mindset must be matched by the philosophy and policies of your school or district. It can be quite overwhelming to be philosophically grounded in the benefits of inclusion if the system in which you work does not support inclusive practices. This incongruence can deplete your self-care efficacy. There are two paths you can take to rectify this dilemma. You can employ your influence and work to enlighten your school or district, or you can find a better-matched system in which to work.

Remember to jot down your scores as a reminder of where you may want to focus your energies. As you contemplate the impact inclusion could have on your self-efficacy, keep in mind these four domains. Think about your connection between self-reflection and the four domains and use that information to guide your professional learning.

CHARTING YOUR INCLUSIVE PRACTICE PATHWAY

Teachers who progress through their careers with an eye on increasing self-efficacy often increase their ability to find success in increasingly inclusive learning environments. Inclusion is not only a source for teacher self-efficacy as one of the Five Thrive Factors, it is also the direct result of increased teacher self-efficacy. When teachers possess higher levels of self-efficacy, they are far more likely to experiment, implement, and lead inclusively. Therefore, the path you have charted for the previous factors serves as your path for increased inclusion.

In this section, you will learn how you can leverage an inclusive framework to either experiment, implement, or lead. The power of inclusion exponentially increases when your school or district has structures in place to allow physical and psychological space for inclusion to flourish. The physical space will be supported through schedules, co-teaching assignments, and universally designed resources. The psychological space will be supported through collaborative professional learning, a universally designed curriculum, and an inclusive vision.

Sometimes a large-scale initiative provides the platform for inclusion leadership. The following example of a Rigor Teamwork Inclusion framework, or RTI Reimagined, provides an example of how one district took a creative approach to empowering inclusion leadership.

All of our students deserve a rigorous and inclusive educational experience supported by collaborative teams of professionals. Sometimes, well-intended research-based practices take on a life of their own and work against these goals. Response to Intervention (RtI) rose to prominence as a multitiered framework to guide the early identification of students needing additional support. The concept of RtI is solid and straightforward. We should be evaluating the effectiveness of our instruction and intervention based on student response as measured by learning data.

Many states adopted it as the official means by which to identify students with specific learning disabilities. Although likely a better solution than previous models, this accelerated the misapplication of RtI principles. Conversations could be heard regularly referring to students as "Tier 2" or "Tier 3" kids. Whenever a new initiative results in more labeling of children, we should be wary.

Most states and educational organizations have expanded the concept of RtI to a more inclusive and broader-based multileveled system of support (MLSS). MLSS considers systems for learning looking far beyond eligibility criteria for receiving intervention. MLSS also applies to social-emotional learning. Some districts still found the shadow of RtI and labeling students lingering in the dialogue in their schools.

Enter RTI Reimagined: Rigor Teamwork Inclusion. The Rigor Teamwork Inclusion model allowed the Hudson School District in Wisconsin, for example, to redefine the dominant discourse around supporting students. This framework requires organizational commitment. The three elements of this model—rigor, teamwork, and inclusion—inform all the decisions regarding advancing the mission of the framework and the district.

Rigor Teamwork Inclusion

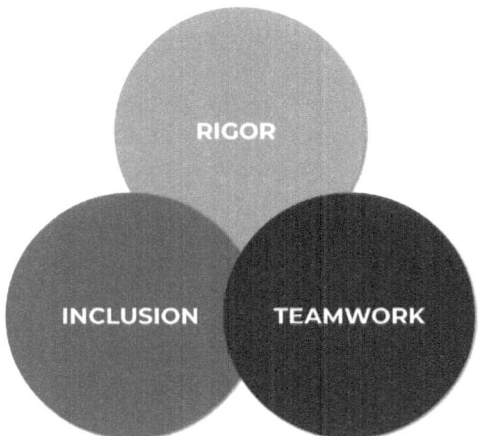

Rigor Teamwork Inclusion. Grambow, Schiltgen, Kovatch, Wheeler, Skoyen, Lotze, Wood, Weinzierl. *Rigor Teamwork Inclusion*. 2021.

DEFINITIONS

- *Rigor:* Challenging standards-based instruction, including opportunities for problem-solving and critical thinking
- *Teamwork:* Breaking down silos and strengthening PLCs with guaranteed access to data for collaborative problem-solving organized by student and by standard
- *Inclusion:* A belief system grounded by concepts of valuing and leveraging individual differences realized by supporting the general education learning environment to meet the needs of all students

THE RIGOR TEAMWORK INCLUSION FORMULAS

The Rigor Teamwork Inclusion model is based on the premise that when all three elements guide decision-making for the support of all students, great results follow. The first three equations demonstrate what happens when one element is missing, while the final describes the value of including all three elements:

- Teamwork + Inclusion: Welcoming environment with watered-down expectations
- Rigor + Inclusion: Unsustainable pockets of excellence
- Rigor + Teamwork: Collaboratively supporting a subset of students
- Rigor + Teamwork + Inclusion: Competent, future-ready global citizenship

OPERATIONALIZING RIGOR TEAMWORK INCLUSION

A district must commit to the first and most important step in operationalizing this: getting the right people at the table. A Rigor Teamwork Inclusion committee should consist of members from all schools and all internal stakeholders who develop inclusive structures and practices. This should include classroom teachers, special educators, interventionists, counselors, psychologists, administrators, specialists, and any other stakeholders who play an integral role in this work. A rule of thumb is to include between 5 and 10 percent of your total certified staff.

You must meet regularly, with the first several meetings focused on developing a shared understanding and inspiring a sense of collective responsibility. These meetings must also include opportunities for the team members to collaborate, share their ideas, and ask tough questions of the leaders. These are heavy meetings that should be scheduled when there is ample time to delve into the paradigm of challenging work. Because of the number of people involved, after-school meetings with childcare and dinner work well.

Next, you must divide the team into workgroups. Not all of the work done with this sort of committee is handled by everyone. Subcommittees are essential. These subcommittees should be designed based on the priorities of the district and the most glaring next steps. For example, you could create teams based on any of the following topics:

- Universal Design for Learning
- Student support teams
- Co-teaching
- Inclusive core strategies
- Inclusive data needs
- Positive Behavioral Interventions and Supports (PBIS)
- In-class interventions
- Classroom community
- Family engagement

You should decide on three to five subcommittees and then offer time to develop long-term and annual goals. Consider the following examples of goals for a co-teaching subcommittee:

- Goal 1: Develop a shared vision and framework for all co-teaching and communicate this vision to all staff members.
- Goal 2: Create structures to support co-teaching, including schedule, planning time, resources, and shared prioritized standards.
- Goal 3: Develop an initial and ongoing professional development structure for new and existing co-teaching partners.

Once you have established your teams, developed a shared, inclusive vision, and clearly defined your goals, you are ready to go! If you have up to 10 percent of your staff working toward goals they developed toward a common, inclusive vision, you can get the flywheel of progress spinning. There is room to experiment, implement, and lead in this model—the recipe for progressing through a thriving career with inclusive growth.

CHAPTER REFLECTIONS

1. How would you describe your experience with inclusive practices?
2. How has your experience with inclusive practices evolved throughout your career?
3. What is your greatest success story with inclusion?
4. How did you feel as a result of that experience?
5. How did that experience impact your self-efficacy? Which of the four domains of teacher self-efficacy was most directly impacted?
6. What conditions make it easier for you to embrace inclusion fully?
7. If you were given the opportunity to develop a district-wide structure to increase inclusion, what would be two priorities?
8. Who would you need to partner with to get this moving?

ACTION PLAN

Now it is time for you to do some planning. Take time to review your action plans from each of the four previous chapters. Connect the dots in your action plans and see where your actions from one plan may support or match steps from another. Connect your action plans to your professional goals. Find partners who are as interested in growing their teacher self-efficacy as you are. You will find more joy in this journey if you travel with friends.

You have all the tools you need to thrive now and throughout your career. You have studied this book and filled your toolbox with everything you need to chart your course. You were called to become teachers. Embrace your talents and gifts, and enjoy your journey toward a long, efficacious, and thriving career.

Appendix: Thrive Tools

The following plans and protocols serve as tools for you to further your examination of the Five Thrive Factors. Approach these tools as a menu at one of the restaurants you stop at along your journey toward a thriving career. Do not read these from beginning to end. Instead, pick and choose based on your personal Thrive profile and your mood.

These tools are also not meant to be an exhaustive collection. They are divided into three sections: thrive action plans, protocols, and discussion techniques. Each section includes a brief description of the purpose of the tools and then a few examples from experts in the field. Peruse the resources, use them as you see fit, search for more from your own go-to professional learning sources, and create your own.

THRIVE ACTION PLANS

You can use these action plans to plot a course for your continued self-efficacy development. For each factor, you have the opportunity to reflect on your current habits and predispositions and then develop a concise and concrete plan for improvement. These tools are not designed to be used consecutively. In fact, they are not all intended to be used by every teacher who reads this book. Find the tools matching your needs.

THRIVE FACTOR ACTION PLAN: SELF-REFLECTION

This document is for you to use to formulate your action plan related to self-reflection. Work through each question step by step. Be vulnerable and honest with yourself in order to maximize the potential benefits to your thriving career. Many of these questions were posed initially in previous chapters. If you took notes while reading, refer to your responses. First, take a moment to jot down your summary scores from the Thrive Inventory.

Personal Thrive Summary Table				
Thrive Factors (Part I)	Score			
	Stage 1	Stage 2	Stage 3	Total
Self-Reflection				
Thrive Domains (Part II)	Score			
Classroom Community Self-Efficacy				
Instruction Self-Efficacy				
Student Engagement Self-Efficacy				
Self-Care Self-Efficacy				

1. How long have you been teaching?
2. Based on what you have read and your results from the Thrive Inventory, how would you describe your stage of self-reflection?
3. Do you gravitate to teacher-focused reflection, student-focused reflection, reflective leadership, or a combination?
4. Where would you like to enhance your self-reflective skills?
5. Which of the four teacher self-efficacy domains do you feel could be supported by your self-reflection? How?
6. What is one thing you can do this week to leverage self-reflection to support your self-efficacy in the domain you identified?

Now take some time to write a SMART goal based on using self-reflection to support your self-efficacy. Here is an example:

I will work with an instructional coach two times per month for the first semester so I can improve student engagement self-efficacy by engaging in student-focused self-reflection. I will measure my improvement by retaking the Thrive Inventory and comparing my scores.

Specific: The teacher knows what they will improve and exactly how they will get there.
Measurable: The teacher indicated the Thrive Inventory will be the measure.
Attainable: The teacher believes they can make this happen.
Relevant: It is explicitly tied to an area of identified need.
Time-bound: The teacher included how often and how long they will engage in the work to meet the goal.

Your turn:
Write your SMART goal by filling in the template:
I will _____ (specific action) _____ (number of times) by/for _____ (date/frequency) so that _____ (reason).

Sometimes developing the measurements can be challenging. It is just fine to have your measurement by your self-evaluation with or without a mini-informal rubric. Start where you are comfortable. Do not let the formality of this process prevent you from giving it a try.

THRIVE FACTOR ACTION PLAN: FEEDBACK

This document is for you to use to formulate your action plan related to feedback. Work through each question step by step. Be vulnerable and honest with yourself to maximize the potential benefits to your thriving career. Some of these questions were initially posed in the previous chapters on feedback. If you took notes while reading, refer to your responses. First, take a moment to jot down your summary scores from the Thrive Inventory.

Personal Thrive Summary Table				
Thrive Factors (Part I)	Score			
	Stage 1	Stage 2	Stage 3	Total
Feedback				
Thrive Domains (Part II)	Score			
Classroom Community Self-Efficacy				
Instruction Self-Efficacy				
Student Engagement Self-Efficacy				
Self-Care Self-Efficacy				

1. How long have you been teaching?
2. Based on what you have read and your results from the Thrive Inventory, how would you describe the stage at which you rely on feedback to support your self-efficacy?
3. Do you gravitate toward feedback from authority figures, feedback from peers, feedback from students, or a combination?
4. What stage do would you want to explore as the next steps for improving your feedback skills?
5. Which of the four teacher self-efficacy domains do you feel could be supported by your feedback? How?
6. What is one thing you can do this week to leverage feedback to support your self-efficacy in your identified domain?

Now take some time to start a SMART goal based on using self-reflection to support your self-efficacy. Here is an example:

I will use a formative assessment practice as a pre-lesson activator two times per week for the first semester so that I can improve my student engagement self-efficacy by gathering feedback directly from students. I will measure my improvement by retaking the Thrive Inventory and comparing my scores.

Specific: The teacher knows what they will improve and exactly how they will get there.
Measurable: The teacher indicated the Thrive Inventory will be the measure.
Attainable: The teacher believes they can make this happen.
Relevant: It is explicitly tied to an area of identified need.
Time-bound: The teacher included how often and how long they will engage in the work to meet the goal.

Your turn:
Write your SMART goal by filling in the template:
I will _____ (specific action) _____ (number of times) by/for _____ (date/frequency) so that _____ (reason).

THRIVE FACTOR ACTION PLAN: COLLABORATION

This document is for you to use to formulate your action plan related to collaboration. Work through each question step by step. Be vulnerable and honest with yourself to maximize the potential benefits to your thriving career. Some of these questions were previously posed in the chapters on collaboration. If you took notes while reading, refer to your responses. First, take a moment to jot down your summary scores from the Thrive Inventory.

Personal Thrive Summary Table				
Thrive Factors (Part I)	**Score**			
	Stage 1	Stage 2	Stage 3	Total
Collaboration				
Thrive Domains (Part II)	**Score**			
Classroom Community Self-Efficacy				
Instruction Self-Efficacy				
Student Engagement Self-Efficacy				
Self-Care Self-Efficacy				

1. How long have you been teaching?
2. Based on what you have read and your results from the Thrive Inventory, how would you describe your stage of collaboration?
3. Do you spend more time being mentored, collaborating with peers outside of the required time, or coaching others? Why?
4. Where would you like to enhance your collaboration skills?
5. Which of the four teacher self-efficacy domains do you feel could be supported by your collaboration? How?
6. What is one thing you can do this week to leverage collaboration to support your self-efficacy in the domain you identified?

Now take some time to write a SMART goal based on using self-reflection to support your self-efficacy. Here is an example:

I will join the Twitter group K12TeacherLeadership @K12TL and participate in two live events per month to improve my classroom community self-efficacy by participating in this peer network. I will measure my improvement by retaking the Thrive Inventory and comparing my scores.

Specific: The teacher knows what they will improve and exactly how they will get there.
Measurable: The teacher indicated the Thrive Inventory will be the measure.
Attainable: The teacher believes they can make this happen.
Relevant: It is explicitly tied to an area of identified need.
Time-bound: The teacher included how often and how long they will engage in the work to meet the goal.

Your turn:
Write your SMART goal by filling in the template:
I will _____ (specific action) _____ (number of times) by/for _____ (date/frequency) so that _____ (reason).

THRIVE FACTOR ACTION PLAN: STUDENT RELATIONSHIPS

This document is for you to use to formulate your action plan related to student relationships. Work through each question step by step. Be vulnerable and honest with yourself to maximize the potential benefits to your thriving career. Many of these questions were initially posed in the chapters on student relationships. If you took notes while reading, refer to your responses. First, take a moment to jot down your summary scores from the Thrive Inventory.

Personal Thrive Summary Table				
Thrive Factors (Part I)	Score			
	Stage 1	Stage 2	Stage 3	Total
Student Relationships				
Thrive Domains (Part II)	Score			
Classroom Community Self-Efficacy				
Instruction Self-Efficacy				
Student Engagement Self-Efficacy				
Self-Care Self-Efficacy				

1. How long have you been teaching?
2. Based on what you have read and your results from the Thrive Inventory, how would you describe how you leverage student relationships to support your self-efficacy?
3. How important to you is it that your students like you?
4. How do you leverage student relationships to build student self-efficacy?
5. Where would you like to enhance your self-reflective skills?
6. Which of the four teacher self-efficacy domains do you feel could be supported by your self-reflection? How?
7. What is one thing you can do this week to leverage self-reflection to support your self-efficacy in the domain you identified?

Now take some time to start a SMART goal based on using self-reflection to support your self-efficacy. Here is an example:

I will build my student engagement self-efficacy by challenging one student per week to move outside of their comfort zone to build their self-efficacy. I will measure my improvement by interviewing the student and gathering data regarding their perceived self-efficacy.

Specific: The teacher knows what they will improve and exactly how they will get there.
Measurable: The teacher indicated the Thrive Inventory will be the measure.
Attainable: The teacher believes they can make this happen.
Relevant: It is explicitly tied to an area of identified need.
Time-bound: The teacher included how often and how long they will engage in the work to meet the goal.

Your turn:
Write your SMART goal by filling in the template:
I will _____ (specific action) _____ (number of times) by/for _____ (date/frequency) so that _____ (reason).

THRIVE FACTOR ACTION PLAN: INCLUSION

This document is for you to use to formulate your action plan related to inclusive practices. Work through each question step by step. Be vulnerable and honest with yourself to maximize the potential benefits to your thriving career. Some of the following questions were initially explored when you explored inclusion. If you took notes while reading, refer to your responses. First, take a moment to jot down your summary scores from the Thrive Inventory.

Personal Thrive Summary Table				
Thrive Factors (Part I)	Score			
	Stage 1	Stage 2	Stage 3	Total
Inclusion				
Thrive Domains (Part II)	Score			
Classroom Community Self-Efficacy				
Instruction Self-Efficacy				
Student Engagement Self-Efficacy				
Self-Care Self-Efficacy				

1. How long have you been teaching?
2. Based on what you have read and your results from the Thrive Inventory, how would you describe the level at which you implement inclusive practices?
3. Do you consider yourself an experimenter, implementer, or leader when it comes to implementing inclusive practices?
4. Where would you like to enhance your inclusive teaching skills?
5. Which of the four teacher self-efficacy domains do you feel could be supported by enhancing your inclusive practice skills? How?
6. What is one thing you can do this week to leverage inclusion to support your self-efficacy in the domain you identified?

Now take some time to write a SMART goal based on using self-reflection to support your self-efficacy. Here is an example:

I will collaborate with my reading specialist to develop a co-teaching model for the three students we share so they do not need to be pulled from my classroom. This will develop my inclusion self-efficacy. By the end of the second trimester, I will reduce the time these students are removed from my class by 50 percent.

Specific: The teacher knows what they will improve and exactly how they will get there.
Measurable: The teacher indicated the Thrive Inventory will be the measure.
Attainable: The teacher believes they can make this happen.

Relevant: It is explicitly tied to an area of identified need.

Time-bound: The teacher included how often and how long they will engage in the work to meet the goal.

Your turn:
Write your SMART goal by filling in the template:

I will _____ (specific action) _____ (number of times) by/for _____ (date/frequency) so that _____ (reason).

PROTOCOLS

A well-developed protocol can energize and focus professional conversation, thus maximizing the impact of any team dialogue. Protocols serve as guides for conversation, guarding against the risk of circular talk lacking tangible outcomes. Each of these protocols can be used by a professional learning community team, a coach, or a principal. The following protocols are designed to guide team conversation focused on the topic of self-efficacy in each of the four Thrive Domains.

PROTOCOL FOR INSTRUCTIONAL SELF-EFFICACY

Protocols for instructional self-efficacy encourage reflection of specific instructional practices and their corresponding impact on student learning. These protocols should include an opportunity to reflect on instruction, compare results to past practice or team members' results, create hypotheses, and take action. The following examples can get you started.

EXAMPLE 1: THE STANDARD PLC PROTOCOL

This protocol is designed to examine student learning data and to make instructional decisions based on that data. The data can come from assessments, work samples, writing samples, or observational notes.

1. What are our norms? (2 minutes)
2. What does this data tell us? What do you notice? (3 minutes)
3. What do we want all students to know or be able to do? (Clarify priority standards and targets of focus.) (2 minutes)
4. How will we know if students have mastered the standards of focus? (What does proficiency look like?) (2 minutes)
5. How will we respond for students who have not yet learned? (Discuss inclusive supports.) (5 minutes)

6. How will we respond for students who have already demonstrated mastery or are ready to do more? (Discuss inclusive supports.) (5 minutes)
7. How is the data similar, and how does the data differ from classroom to classroom? (8 minutes)
8. So what's the plan? What are you going to do tomorrow? What are you going to do this month? What are you going to do differently next year? (8 minutes)

(Based on DuFour's Four Questions for PLCs.)

EXAMPLE 2: THE FRAMING CONSULTANCY PROTOCOL[1]

This protocol is designed to allow one team member to think deeply about an instructional dilemma and receive feedback and advice from a consultancy group, often a PLC team.

These first four steps are in preparation for the actual protocol. This protocol was adapted from the work of the School Reform Initiative (SRI), an independent, nonprofit organization dedicated to educational equity and excellence. Thousands of teachers and school leaders have relied on SRI for support and their resources. They are well known for their catalog of protocols.[2]

- Think About Your Dilemma
  A dilemma is a problem that is perplexing and does not have a definite right or wrong answer. Clarify the actual dilemma that is on your mind.

- Reflectively Write About Your Dilemma
  Writing is thinking. Take some to write about your dilemma to further clarify your thinking. Consider some of these questions to guide your writing:
  o Why is this a dilemma for you?
  o Why is this dilemma vital to you?
  o If you could take a snapshot of this dilemma, what would you/we see?
  o What have you done already to try to remedy or manage the dilemma?
  o What were the results of those efforts?

- Frame a Focus Question for Your Consultancy Group
  o Try to pose a question around the dilemma seeming to you to get to the heart of the matter.
  o Remember the question you pose will guide the consultancy group in their discussion of the dilemma.

- Critique Your Focus Question
  o Is this question important to my practice?
  o Is this question important to student learning?
  o Is this question important to others in my profession?

PROCESS

1. The presenter provides an overview of the dilemma they are struggling with and frames a question for the consultancy group to consider. The focus of the group's conversation is on the dilemma. (10–15 minutes)
2. The consultancy group asks clarifying questions of the presenter that would have brief, factual answers. (5 minutes)
3. The group asks probing questions of the presenter. These questions should be worded to help the presenter clarify and expand their thinking about the dilemma presented to the consultancy group. The goal here is for the presenter to learn more about the question they framed and analyze the dilemma presented. The presenter responds to the group's questions. At the end of the 10 minutes, the facilitator asks the presenter to restate their group questions. (10 minutes)
4. The group talks with each other about the dilemma presented. In this step, the group works to define the issues more thoroughly and objectively. Sometimes group members suggest actions the presenter might consider taking; if they do, these should be framed as "open suggestions" and should be made only after the group has thoroughly analyzed the dilemma. The presenter doesn't speak during this discussion but listens in and takes notes. The group talks about the presenter in the third person. (15 minutes) Possible questions to frame the discussion:
   a. What did we hear?
   b. What didn't we hear that might be relevant?
   c. What assumptions seem to be in play?
   d. What questions have been raised for us?
5. The presenter reflects on what they heard and what they are now thinking, sharing anything that particularly resonated for them during any part of the consultancy with the group. (5 minutes)
6. The facilitator leads a brief conversation about the group's observation of the consultancy process. (5 minutes)

PROTOCOL FOR CLASSROOM CULTURE SELF-EFFICACY

Protocols for classroom culture self-efficacy are the most complex as they can challenge the core beliefs of teachers. These protocols should force us to broaden our perspectives, challenge our biases, and reflect deeply on our practices. The examples below accomplish all of this brilliantly.

EXAMPLE #1: THE COLLABORATIVE ASSESSMENT CONFERENCE PROTOCOL

According to the originator of the protocol, Steve Seidel, this protocol serves four functions, aiming to:

1. Enhance teachers' perceptions of their students' work;
2. Encourage depth of perception by demonstrating all which can be seen in student work;
3. Encourage a balance of perception by focusing on strengths and needs; and
4. Encourage dialogue among teachers.

Number of Participants: 5–15 participants, a presenter, and a facilitator
Time Required: 45–90 minutes

PROCESS

Presenting. The facilitator begins by asking the presenting teacher what they brought for the group to examine. The teacher presents a single student work artifact offering minimal context.

Describing the work. The facilitator asks, "What do you see?" Participants respond without making judgments about the quality of the work or their personal preferences. If judgments emerge, the facilitator asks the speaker to describe the evidence that informed the judgment.

Raising questions. The facilitator asks, "What questions does this work raise for you?" Group members ask any questions about the work, the child, the assignment, the circumstances of the work, and so forth that have come up for them during the previous steps of the conference. The presenting teacher makes notes but does not yet respond.

Speculating. The facilitator asks, "What do you think this student is working on?" Based on their reading or observation of the work, participants offer their ideas.

Responding. The facilitator invites the presenting teacher to speak: "After hearing all this, what are your thoughts?" This is the presenter's opportunity to respond, provide context and perspective, and share ideas about the student work.

Reflecting and Discussing. The facilitator invites open discussion asking the participants to reflect on their experiences using the protocol in the larger context of teaching and learning experiences. Questions could probe the participants about what they found useful or challenging.

PROTOCOL FOR SELF-CARE

This simple protocol can help you prioritize your well-being.

EXAMPLE # 2: CONSTRUCTIVIST LISTENING DYAD

Purpose: To help participants become better at talking in-depth with others and become more attentive in the process.

Details: This protocol is designed for dyads (two people) to listen to each other. Often this will take place with several dyads in a room. The following guidelines form the basis for the communication in this process.

- Each person is given equal time to talk about whatever they choose to talk about. The talker may not criticize or complain about the listener or mutual colleagues.
- The listener must listen intently and may not break in with their perspective or interpret, paraphrase, analyze, or give advice.
- What is said and heard stays completely confidential.

STEPS

1. *Setting the focus.* The facilitator begins by explaining the purpose of listening in a constructivist dyad is to benefit the talker. They clarify that the power of the process depends on the partners dedicating themselves to the power of listening. To help participants grasp the point, the facilitator may engage them in some preliminary discussion based on prompts like, "When you have felt listened to, how did it feel? What was its value to you?"
2. *Setting the time.* Next, the facilitator sets the listening duration anywhere from 2 minutes for a practice round to 10 minutes for a regular round among experienced dyads.
3. *Dyads proceed.* Dyads talk and listen according to the guidelines.
4. *Reflection.* The facilitator leads a general discussion of the process. Prompts might include: What came up for you? How did you feel as a listener? How did you feel as a talker? What benefit did you gain as a talker? What was difficult for you? What came up for you while reflecting on the topic?

Provide structured reminders about the importance of self-care. Use this protocol during a school day when you have about 5 minutes and feel like you need to reconnect with your priorities.

PROCESS

1. Think of one student who made you happy today.
2. Set a "go-home" time and stick to it!
3. Plan the first three things that you are going to do when you are home and make sure that they help you feel grounded and at ease.
4. Carve out at least 15 minutes for yourself and 15 minutes for you and a loved one and make sure you make those precious 30 minutes a priority.
5. Find the student who made you happy today and tell them why.

Appendix: Thrive Tools

DISCUSSION TECHNIQUES

Discussion and dialogue are critical components of any thriving teacher's classroom and professional practice. In the book *Discussion as a Way of Teaching*, Stephen Brookfield and Stephen Preskill identify four purposes of discussion. They are to:

1. Help participants reach a more critically informed understanding about the topic or topics under consideration;
2. Enhance participants' self-awareness and their capacity for self-critique;
3. Foster an appreciation among participants for the diversity of opinion that invariably emerges when viewpoints are exchanged openly and honestly; and
4. Act as a catalyst to helping people take informed action in the world.[3]

I have found many valuable resources for encouraging dialogue and discussion among students and adults. Here are just a few:

Tools for Adult Dialogue

- *The Discussion Book*, Brookfield, and Preskill, 2016. This is a wonderfully practical book, chock-full of dialogue-inspiring techniques. You will waste no time in reaping the benefits of this fantastic collection of discussion techniques.[4]
- School Reform Initiative at https://www.schoolreforminitiative.org/ offers a plethora of tools to encourage deep and meaningful adult dialogue.[5]

Tools for Student Dialogue

- *Discussion as a Way of Teaching*, Brookfield and Preskill, 2005. Much like *The Discussion Book*, the strategies Brookfield and Preskill explore in this book could effectively be used with adults or children.[6] The authors offer a compelling argument for the use of dialogue to empower all students. They complement this argument with concrete examples.
- We Are Teachers @Weareteachers.com is a great place to go for practical ideas ready for the classroom. Their 2014 post on discussion strategies called "13 Strategies to Improve Classroom Discussion (Plus Anchor Charts)" is a great place to start if you are looking for discussion ideas and are short on time. It can be found at https://www.weareteachers.com/13-strategies-to-improve-student-classroom-discussions/.[7]

General Tools for Teachers and Coaches

- "How Well Do I Know My Students?" Go to https://bit.ly/3DUc0uI for a fillable form.
- "Coaches Collaboration Coordination Tool," https://bit.ly/2ZiXqOf.

How Well Do I Know My Students?		
\multicolumn{3}{l}{List your students in the first column as they come to your mind. Avoid alphabetical order or a seating chart. Just print the names as they come to mind. In the middle column, write one thing you know the child genuinely enjoys. In the third column, indicate with a checkmark if you are certain the student knows you know this about them.}		
Student Name	**One Thing I Know About Them**	**Do They Know I Know?**

Coaches Collaboration Coordination Tool

Directions: Use this collaboration coordination tool to identify opportunities for collaborative coaching. Reflect on the goals, interests, and responsibilities of the teachers with whom you work. List them in the appropriate column. Be brief in your descriptions. Once the form is filled out, you can sort it by any columns to find collaboration opportunities.

Teacher	Goals	Interests	Responsibilities

Notes

CHAPTER 1

1. National Commission on Excellence, *A Nation at Risk: The Imperative for Educational Reform* (Washington, DC: National Commission on Excellence in Education, 1983).
2. Wisconsin State Legislature, "Wisconsin Budget Repair Bill," 2011 Wisconsin Act 10 (Madison: Wisconsin State Legislature).
3. Albert Bandura, *Self-Efficacy: The Exercise of Control* (New York: W. H. Freeman, 1997), 92.
4. Bandura, *Self-Efficacy*, 92.
5. Ibid.
6. Megan Tschannen-Moran and Anita Woolfolk Hoy, "Teacher Efficacy: Capturing an Elusive Construct," *Teaching and Teacher Education* 17, no. 7 (2001): 783–805, https://doi.org/10.1016/s0742-051x(01)00036-1.
7. Adapted from Tschannen-Moran and Woolfolk Hoy, "Teacher Efficacy," 788.

CHAPTER 3

1. J. K. Rowling, *Harry Potter and the Goblet of Fire* (New York: Bloomsbury Children's, 2000).
2. Kurt Lewin, *Resolving Social Conflicts and Field Theory in Social Science* (New York: American Psychologocial Association, 1997), 288.
3. Pete Hall and Alisa A. Simeral, *Building Teachers' Capacity for Success: A Collaborative Approach for Coaches and School Leaders* (Alexandria, VA: Association for Supervision and Curriculum Development, 2008), 40.
4. Hall and Simeral, *Building Teachers' Capacity for Success*, 40.
5. Hall and Simeral, *Building Teachers' Capacity for Success*, 41.
6. Donald A. Schön, *Educating the Reflective Practitioner* (San Francisco: Jossey-Bass, 1987).
7. Tom Schulman, *Dead Poets Society*, directed by Peter Weir, starring Robin Williams (Burbank, CA: Touchstone Pictures, 1989).
8. Ramón Menéndez, *Stand and Deliver* (Burbank, CA: Warner Bros., 1988).

9. Jay Mathews, *Escalante: The Best Teacher in America* (New York: Henry Holt, 1988), 191.

10. Mathews, *Escalante*, 310.

11. Henry Gradillas and Jerry Jesness, *Standing and Delivering* (Lanham, MD: Rowman & Littlefield Education, 2010), 77.

12. Dave Rybaczewski, *Beatles Book*, accessed June 4, 2020, http://www.beatlesebooks.com/i-feel-fine.

13. Douglas Stone and Sheila Heen, *Thanks for the Feedback: The Science and Art of Receiving Feedback Well* (London: Portfolio Penguin, 2019), 29.

14. Stone and Heen, *Thanks for the Feedback*, 102.

CHAPTER 4

1. Rob Phillips and Jay Korreck, *Teacher of the Year* (Raleigh, NC: At Large Productions, 2017).

2. Sean Schat, "Exploring Care in Education," *International Christian Community of Teacher Educators Journal* 13, no. 2 (2018): 1–10.

3. Schat, "Exploring Care in Education."

4. Schat, "Exploring Care in Education." Used with permission.

5. Andrea Zampetopoulos, Tammy Potter, and Karen Krey, replies to "How Well Do You Know Your Students?" Responsive Classroom (online forum), https://www.responsiveclassroom.org/how-well-do-you-know-your-students/.

6. Laura Lundy, "'Voice' Is Not Enough: Conceptualising Article 12 of the United Nations Convention on the Rights of the Child," *British Educational Research Journal* 33, no. 6 (2007): 927–42, https://doi.org/10.1080/01411920701657033.

7. Adapted from Lundy, "'Voice' Is Not Enough."

8. Inclusive Education Canada, "What Is Inclusive Education?" https://inclusiveeducation.ca/about/what-is-ie/.

9. UNICEF, "Inclusive Education: Every Child Has the Right to Quality Education and Learning," https://www.unicef.org/education/inclusive-education.

10. Wendy Murawski and Wendy Lochner, *Beyond Co-Teaching Basics: A Data-Driven, No-Fail Model for Continuous Improvement* (Alexandria, VA: ASCD, 2018).

11. Murawski and Lochner, *Beyond Co-Teaching Basics*, 19.

12. Murawski and Lochner, *Beyond Co-Teaching Basics*, 18.

13. CAST, "About Universal Design for Learning," https://www.cast.org/impact/universal-design-for-learning-udl.

CHAPTER 5

1. Global Self-Care Federation, "Who We Are, Vision, Mission and Work Focus," https://www.selfcarefederation.org/.

2. Stephen R. Covey, A. Roger Merrill, and Rebecca R. Merrill, *First Things First: To Live, to Love, to Learn, to Leave a Legacy* (New York: Simon and Schuester, 1994), 37.

3. Covey, Merrill, and Merrill, *First Things First*, 37

4. Covey, Merrill, and Merrill, *First Things First*, 37. Adapted from the work of Stephen R. Covey.
5. Covey, Merrill, and Merrill, *First Things First*, 38.
6. Covey, Merrill, and Merrill, *First Things First*, 38.
7. Angela Scioli, email interview by David Grambow, December 19, 2020.

CHAPTER 6

1. Megan Tschannen-Moran and Anita Woolfolk Hoy, "Teacher Efficacy: Capturing an Elusive Construct," *Teaching and Teacher Education* 17, no. 7 (2001): 783–805, https://doi.org/10.1016/s0742-051x(01)00036-1.
2. Based on the work of Tschannen-Moran and Woolfolk Hoy, "Teacher Efficacy."
3. Based on concepts developed by Tschannen-Moran and Woolfolk Hoy, "Teacher Efficacy."
4. Ibid.

CHAPTER 7

1. Diane Sweeney, *Student-Centered Coaching at the Secondary Level* (Thousand Oaks, CA: Corwin, 2010), 6.
2. Red4EdNC, "The Red4EdNC Story and Why We Are Archiving This Site," https://www.red4ednc.com/.
3. Red4EdNC.

CHAPTER 8

1. Dick Wolf, *Law & Order*, NBC (Universal City, CA: Wolf Entertainment, 1990).

CHAPTER 9

1. Kelly M. Hannum, *Social Identity: Knowing Yourself, Leading Others* (London: Center for Creative Leadership, 2007), 12.
2. Liana Loewus, "Why Teachers Leave—or Don't: A Look at the Numbers," *Education Week*, May 4, 2021, https://www.edweek.org/teaching-learning/why-teachers-leave-or-dont-a-look-at-the-numbers/2021/05.
3. Lucinda Gray and Soheyla Taie, "Public School Teacher Attrition and Mobility in the First Five Years," NCES 2015-337 (April 2015), US Department of Education, Institute of Education Sciences (IES), National Center for Education Statistics (NCES), https://nces.ed.gov/pubs2015/2015337.pdf.
4. US Department of Education, "Facts about the Teaching Profession for A National Conversation About Teaching," IES NCES, accessed July 9, 2020, http://www.mnase.org/uploads/4/7/7/9/47793163/peg_16teaching-profession-facts.pdf.

5. Emma García and Elaine Weiss, "The Teacher Shortage Is Real, Large and Growing, and Worse Than We Thought," Economic Policy Institute (EPI), March 26, 2019, https://www.epi.org/publication/the-teacher-shortage-is-real-large-and-growing-and-worse-than-we-thought-the-first-report-in-the-perfect-storm-in-the-teacher-labor-market-series/.

6. SocialEmotionalLearning, @SELearningEDU (2021), accessed August 10, 2021, https://twitter.com/selearningedu?lang=en.

7. Brené Brown, "Brené Brown on Empathy," December 10, 2013, YouTube, https://www.youtube.com/watch?v=1Evwgu369Jw.

8. CASEL (Collaborative for Academic, Social, and Emotional Learning), CASEL Home page, "Events and Webinars," accessed May 21, 2020, https://casel.org/events-webinars/.

CHAPTER 10

1. Responsive Classroom, "About Responsive Classroom," accessed February 27, 2020, https://www.responsiveclassroom.org/about/.

APPENDIX

1. School Reform Initiative, "Protocols," accessed April 15, 2020, https://www.schoolreforminitiative.org/protocols/.

2. Ibid.

3. Stephen D. Brookfield and Stephen Preskill, *Discussion as a Way of Teaching: Tools and Techniques for Democractic Classrooms* (San Francisco: Jossey-Bass, 2005).

4. Stephen D. Brookfield and Stephen Preskill, *The Discussion Book: 50 Great Ways to Get People Talking* (San Francisco: Jossey-Bass, 2016).

5. School Reform Initiative, "Protocols."

6. Brookfield and Preskill, *The Discussion Book*, 39.

7. We Are Teachers Staff, " Classroom Ideas: 13 Strategies to Improve Student Classroom Discussions (Plus Anchor Charts)," October 16, 2014, https://www.weareteachers.com/13-strategies-to-improve-student-classroom-discussions/.

About the Author

David E. Grambow, EdD, serves as an assistant superintendent for teaching and learning in Hudson, Wisconsin. He has previously enjoyed serving as a principal, a classroom teacher, and special educator. He conducts leadership seminars for aspiring principals and has previously consulted with school districts throughout the United States on classroom community and school culture. David has three wonderful children with his wife, Lori, and three grandchildren. In addition to his passion for education and his family, David enjoys guitars, dogs, and Wisconsin supper clubs.

www.ingramcontent.com/pod-product-compliance
Lightning Source LLC
Chambersburg PA
CBHW030121240426
43673CB00041B/1358